THE BEST

Includes all the recipes from the TV series
Silvana Franco, Paul Merrett and Ben O'Donoghue

This book is published to accompany the television series entitled
The Best, which was first broadcast in 2002.
The series was produced by Endemol UK Productions for BBC Television.
Executive Producer: Janice Gabriel
Series Producer: Sue Walton
Directors: Stuart Bateup and Claudia Lewis
Home Economist: Karen Taylor
Production Manager: Lesley Bywater
Production Co-ordinator: Sarah Kershaw
Project Manager: Frances Goddard

Published by BBC Worldwide Ltd, 80 Wood Lane, London W12 0TT
First published 2002
Text copyright © Silvana Franco, Paul Merrett, Ben O'Donoghue 2002
The moral right of the authors has been asserted.

ISBN 0 563 48853 0

Photographs by Gareth Morgans © BBC Worldwide Ltd 2002, except
page 77 (bottom right) by Geoff Wilkinson © BBC Worldwide Ltd 2001

Commissioning Editor: Nicky Copeland
Project Editor: Julia Zimmermann
Copy Editor: Deborah Savage
Cover Art Director: Pene Parker
Book Art Director: Lisa Pettibone
Designer: Sarah Jackson
Home Economists: Lorna Brash and David Morgan
Stylist: Hélène Lesur
Production Controller: Kenneth McKay

Set in Univers and Eurostile
Printed and bound in Great Britain by Butler & Tanner Ltd, Frome, Somerset
Jacket printed by Lawrence Allen Ltd, Weston-super-Mare
Colour origination by Kestrel Digital Colour Ltd, Chelmsford, Essex

CONTENTS

THE BEST CHEFS...

Name: Paul Merrett
Age: 34
Cooking credentials: Following an apprenticeship at The Ritz, Paul trained under Peter Kromberg at Le Soufflé and Gary Rhodes at The Greenhouse, Mayfair. As Head Chef at the Meridien Hotel in Piccadilly Circus, he established a reputation for having a style of cooking that reflects both his European training and a childhood spent on the East African spice island of Zanzibar. Paul's food continued to achieve rave reviews at Interlude in Charlotte Street, culminating in the award of a Michelin star.
Current occupation: Paul has now returned to The Greenhouse as Head Chef.
Favourite food: Chicken Biriani.
Pet hates: Cutting corners just to save time.
Greatest triumph on *The Best*: Coming back from 4–0 down.

Name: Silvana Franco
Age: 33
Cooking credentials: Silvana is a food writer and stylist with over a decade's experience of working in the food media. She was senior writer on *BBC Good Food* and worked as Food Editor for the *M&S Magazine*, before entering the world of television as a stylist and writer on *Can't Cook Won't Cook*, *Ainsley Harriott's Meals in Minutes*, *Ainsley's Barbecue Bible* and *Gourmet Express 1* and *2*.
Current occupation: Silvana now runs her own company, Fork, together with two other food writers.
Favourite food: Her mum's spaghetti.
Pet hates: Fussy dishes that get you in a flap when you cook.
Greatest triumph on *The Best*: Winning with *Raspberry Cheesecake Tart*.

Name: Ben O'Donoghue
Age: 32
Cooking credentials: Ben started off his career working in several different restaurants throughout Australia, including Jessica's in Perth, and the much acclaimed Goodfella's restaurant in the trendy Newtown area of Sydney. He spent several years at The River Café and has been a consultant and food stylist to Jamie Oliver since January 1998, as well as assisting him with various outside catering functions. These include cooking for Tony Blair and the Italian Prime Minister at 10 Downing Street last year.
Current occupation: Ben is now Head Chef at the exclusive Monte's Club in Knightsbridge.
Favourite food: Anything wild.
Pet hates: Supermarkets.
Greatest triumph on *The Best*: Winning with *Chinese Pork and Egg Congee*.

THE BEST CHALLENGE...

What happens when two top chefs and one experienced cook all pit their wits against each other to find the very best recipes? The BBC decided to find out…

The Best brought Paul Merrett, Ben O'Donoghue and Silvana Franco together in the same kitchen and let them compete to find the best recipes in categories ranging from The Best Sandwich to The Best Quick Chocolate Pudding. Silvana has a no-nonsense approach to cooking and a genius for store-cupboard shortcuts. Ben likes to use only the freshest ingredients but assembles his dishes in his characteristically laid-back Aussie style. Paul is no fan of shortcuts but instead believes that time, effort, and attention to detail pay dividends when it comes to cooking. Each of them thought that their recipes would be the best. The decision-makers? A panel of food-loving judges, waiting in the next-door dining room to receive each dish anonymously through the service hatch and give their verdict via text message to the anxious trio in the kitchen…

Now it's up to you to decide which recipes are truly *The Best*.

SERVES 2

3 ripe peaches

500 g (1 lb 2 oz) caster sugar

1 litre (1¾ pints) still mineral water

rind of 1 lemon, peeled in strips with a peeler (lemon then halved for juicing)

2 vanilla pods, split

½ cinnamon stick

1 star anise

3 eggs

2 tablespoons milk

2 large slices or 4 smaller slices of panettone, cut in half diagonally

25 g (1 oz) unsalted butter

caster sugar and ground cinnamon, to taste

extra-thick double cream, to serve

Ben's PANETTONE AND POACHED PEACHES

French toast or 'eggy bread' can seem pretty boring, but this version has everything you need to make that weekend breakfast special. Sweet, spicy panettone drenched in a sweet egg wash, gently fried in butter and topped with fresh poached peaches and cream – awesome!

1 First poach the peaches. Put the sugar in a medium-size pan and pour over the mineral water. Add the lemon rind and a squeeze of juice, vanilla pods, cinnamon stick and star anise. Cook over a low heat, stirring occasionally, until the sugar has dissolved. Bring to the boil and boil rapidly for 5 minutes. Remove from the heat, add the peaches and place a plate on top of them to keep the peaches immersed in the sugar syrup. Leave until cold. When cooled, remove the peaches and peel. Halve them and remove the stones. Cut the flesh into slices.

2 Meanwhile, prepare the panettone. Whisk the eggs and milk together in a shallow dish. Soak the panettone slices in the egg mixture for 1 minute, turning once. Melt the butter in a small frying pan and gently pan-fry the bread for 1–2 minutes on each side, until golden brown. Remove and drain on kitchen paper.

3 Sprinkle with caster sugar and cinnamon to taste.

4 Serve the eggy bread topped with the poached peaches. Drizzle a little syrup over and serve with a dollop of double cream.

Paul's
PINEAPPLE CARPACCIO AND SORBET

SERVES 4–6

2 stems of lemongrass

300 ml (10 fl oz) milk

300 g (10 oz) caster sugar

4 teaspoons liquid glucose (available from chemists)

3 green cardamom pods, smashed

2 vanilla pods, split

400 g (14 oz) Greek yoghurt

75 ml (2 1/2 fl oz) double cream

1 small–medium pineapple

Chefs rarely have anything for breakfast except for a cup of strong coffee. In the kitchen we eat lunch at 10.30 am because, by noon, we are cooking for customers. But very occasionally I'll push the breakfast boat out on a Sunday. This is real summer breakfast stuff and the sorbet alone will make the cost of an ice-cream machine a worthwhile investment. Choose only the ripest pineapple.

1 Remove any tough outer leaves from the lemongrass and discard. Smash the lemongrass stalk with a rolling pin, then cut into 2–3 pieces. Put the milk, sugar and glucose into a small pan and bring to the boil. Add the lemongrass, cardamom and vanilla pods and bring back to the boil. Remove from the heat and allow to cool.

2 Strain through a fine sieve into a large bowl and then stir in the Greek yoghurt and cream. Pour the mixture into the ice-cream machine and churn until thick and creamy. The sorbet is now ready to serve or, alternatively, turn it into a suitable container and store in the freezer for up to 2 months.

3 Next, prepare the pineapple. Cut off the leafy top and slice off the base. Cut in half lengthways and remove the core. Peel the pineapple and slice the flesh very thinly with a sharp knife.

4 Arrange the pineapple slices, slightly overlapping, on individual serving plates. Top with a scoop of the sorbet.

MAKES 12 MUFFINS

- 300 g (10 oz) plain white flour
- 2 teaspoons baking powder
- 150 g (5 oz) light brown sugar
- 85 g (3 oz) pecans, roughly chopped
- 1 egg
- 1 teaspoon vanilla extract
- 225 ml (8 fl oz) milk
- 50 g (2 oz) butter, melted
- 4 tablespoons strong black coffee or Espresso
- 2 tablespoons small sugar crystals or granulated demerara sugar

COFFEE AND PECAN MUFFINS

These tasty muffins make a yummy breakfast (or mid-morning snack, and they're good with a frothy hot chocolate in the afternoon). If, like me, you can't eat breakfast until a good hour after you've woken up, these are perfect for making the day before, slipping into your pocket on the way out of the door and eating on the bus to work. And they're so simple to make, they're great even for those who usually shy away from baking.

1 Preheat the oven to 200°C/400°F/Gas Mark 6. Sift the flour and baking powder into a large bowl and stir in the sugar and pecans.

2 Crack the egg into a separate bowl and whisk in the vanilla, milk, melted butter and coffee.

3 Stir the liquid into the dry ingredients, taking care not to over mix. Spoon the mixture into a 12-hole muffin tin, lined with circles of greaseproof paper.

4 Scatter over the sugar crystals and bake for 15–20 minutes, until well risen and just firm.

SERVES 1

100 g (4 oz) shelled fresh peas

a small handful of fresh mint leaves

30 g (1¼ oz) grated young pecorino cheese

30 g (1¼ oz) Parmesan cheese, finely grated

a squeeze of fresh lemon juice

1 tablespoon olive oil

25 g (1 oz) unsalted butter

3 free-range eggs

1–2 tablespoons crème fraîche

salt and freshly ground black pepper

Ben's

PEA AND MINT FRITTATA

What better way to enjoy an egg but as a wonderfully light, summery Italian-style omelette? The English summer provides the perfect flavours to accompany it – peas and mint – tasty and visually stunning. I like to use free-range Old Cotswold Legbar eggs in the recipe for perfect results again and again!

1 Preheat the oven to 180°C/350°F/Gas Mark 4.

2 Plunge the peas into boiling water for 1–2 minutes to soften or, if small and sweet, just wash. Drain and place in a pestle and mortar with the roughly chopped mint (reserving a few leaves for garnishing) and grated pecorino and pound to a paste. Alternatively, lightly blitz the pea mixture in a food processor. Add some salt, half the Parmesan, a squeeze of lemon juice and the olive oil.

3 Melt the butter in a non-stick, ovenproof frying pan. Break the eggs into a bowl, mix lightly, add a splash of water and season with salt and freshly ground black pepper. Add the mixture to the pan and then fold in two-thirds of the pea mixture. Stir, loosening the cooked egg from the sides of the pan until the eggs start to thicken.

4 Place the crème fraîche in the middle, with the remaining pea mixture, and bake in the oven for 3 minutes until just set.

5 Carefully slide the frittata on to a plate. Serve sprinkled with the reserved mint and the remaining Parmesan.

Paul's
PERFECT CHEESE SOUFFLÉ

This cheese (Tête de Moine) soufflé with Parmesan crust is served with a watercress and fennel salad. Soufflés have a reputation for being tricky and unpredictable but follow a reliable recipe and they work every time. Here's a great savoury soufflé recipe to get you started. You may have to shop around a bit at cheese markets for the Swiss Tête de Moine cheese but, if you can't find it, Gruyère or Parmesan are fine as a substitute. It makes a great starter or vegetarian main course and I bet, once you've mastered this one, you'll be as fascinated by soufflés as I am.

1 Preheat the oven to 180°C/350°F/Gas Mark 4. Preheat the grill. Soften 25 g (1 oz) of the butter and use to grease eight 175 ml (6 fl oz) ramekins lightly. Sprinkle with 25 g (1 oz) of the grated Parmesan cheese to coat evenly.

2 Pour the milk into a large saucepan, add the remaining butter and bring to the boil.

3 Meanwhile, whisk together the flour, egg yolks and whole eggs with an electric whisk for about 2–3 minutes, until you have a thick custard. Pour the hot milk over the custard and stir until well combined. Return the mixture to the pan and cook, stirring constantly, for 3–4 minutes over a low heat. If necessary, return to the bowl and whisk again to ensure the mixture is thick and smooth.

4 Turn the mixture into a bowl and add the Tête de Moine cheese and the remaining grated Parmesan. Season with salt and pepper.

5 Whisk the egg whites to soft peaks. Gently fold into the sauce, using a large metal spoon. Divide the mixture between the ramekins. Place on a baking sheet and pop under the grill for 1 minute or until the tops start to go golden brown. This will make sure that you get that lovely straight up rise. Bake for 8–12 minutes, until risen.

6 Meanwhile, trim the base of the fennel, halve and very thinly slice, then toss with the watercress, balsamic vinegar and olive oil. Serve with the hot soufflés.

SERVES 8

85 g (3 oz) softened butter

50 g (2 oz) Parmesan cheese, finely grated

300 ml (10 fl oz) full-fat or semi-skimmed milk

65 g (2½ oz) plain white flour

6 free-range eggs, separated, plus 2 free-range eggs left whole

85 g (3 oz) Tête de Moine cheese, grated

salt and freshly ground white pepper

For the accompanying salad:

1 fennel bulb

a small bunch of watercress, about 50 g (2 oz)

1 tablespoon balsamic vinegar

2 tablespoons extra-virgin olive oil

16

Silvana's

CURRIED SCRAMBLED EGGS

Eggs respond very well to being livened up with some exciting curry flavours. This is my perfect home-alone TV dinner; it takes minutes to prepare and goes down brilliantly with a cold glass of light lager.

1 Preheat the oven to 200°C/400°F/Gas Mark 6. Place the naan bread on a baking sheet and pop into the oven for 5 minutes to warm through. Alternatively, heat on a griddle.

2 Place the butter in a smallish non-stick frying pan. Add the spring onions to the pan, with the cumin seeds, and cook for 1 minute or so until beginning to soften.

3 Meanwhile, crack the eggs into a bowl and lightly whisk together with the curry paste, 2 tablespoons of cold water and some salt and pepper. Pour into the pan and leave to set for a minute or two.

4 Continue to cook for another couple of minutes, stirring until almost set. Stir in the coriander leaves then spoon on to the warm naan and serve immediately.

SERVES 1

1 naan bread

a large knob of butter

2 spring onions, thinly sliced

a pinch of cumin seeds

3 eggs

1–2 teaspoons curry paste

a handful of fresh coriander leaves

salt and freshly ground black pepper

3 BEST SCRAMBLED EGG TIPS

BEN For the best scrambled eggs, mix three of the best-quality eggs per person in a bowl and season with salt and pepper. Then get some butter gently foaming in a saucepan before adding the eggs. When it's almost cooked but still wet, turn the heat off and add a dollop of cream. Scrambled eggs can be really special so I always serve them with truffle flavoured pecorino cheese on toast.

PAUL I beat my eggs, preferably organic ones, when they're in the pan and you get the best results with a fork. Then I add a knob of butter and cook on a low heat, using a wooden spoon to stir. I add a bit of milk to stop them cooking and simply season with salt and pepper for the perfect scrambled eggs.

SILVANA I break my eggs straight into the pan, a small frying pan is best. I never whisk my eggs beforehand either because it can curdle them. I like them to set so the yolk and white are quite separate, which is why I use a chopstick for stirring because you can ripple the eggs without disturbing them too much. I like to finish them off with black pepper and a bit of grated Parmesan.

SERVES 6

500 g (1 lb 2 oz) minced lamb

2 tablespoons roughly chopped fresh marjoram

4 tablespoons roughly chopped fresh flatleaf parsley

1 red onion, very finely chopped

salt and freshly ground black pepper

To serve:

Moroccan hob loaf (or a flat loaf topped with sesame seeds)

extra-virgin olive oil, to drizzle

ground cumin, to sprinkle

pickled chillies or fresh red chillies

1 red onion, thinly sliced

3 tomatoes, sliced

Ben's

LAMB KOFTA SANDWICH

Travelling through Morocco, I ate in many souks and so often was sensually inspired by the sights, sounds and smells of that wonderful country. This sandwich is something I had after encountering a camel butcher – but, to make it more appealing to the judges of the show, I substituted lamb mince for the camel. It was the simplicity of flavours and the do-it-yourself construction that did it for me, along with the idea of a group of mates tucking in to the koftas.

1 You will need 12 skewers. If using wooden kebab sticks, soak in water for 30 minutes before using. Mix together the lamb mince, marjoram, flatleaf parsley, red onion and salt and pepper. Divide the mixture into 24 equal-size balls. Squish two balls on to each skewer. Chill until ready to use, using your hands to make two flat oval shapes.

2 Heat a large grill plate or pan (large enough to take the skewers) and brush with oil. Or preheat the grill. Lay the skewers on and cook for 4–5 minutes, turning occasionally, until browned on all sides.

3 Cut the loaf into wedges and toast on the grill plate or under the grill for a minute or so. Sprinkle with olive oil and put in the centre of the table, with the lamb koftas, ground cumin, salt, chillies, red onion and tomatoes. Let everyone sprinkle their bread with a little ground cumin, add as much or as little of the pickled or fresh chilli, red onion and tomatoes as they like, then simply place the kofta on top and gently pull out the skewer; then tuck in and enjoy!

Paul's
CLASSIC CRAB CLUB SANDWICH

SERVES 3–4

5 rashers unsmoked streaky dry-cure bacon

1 small white crusty bloomer loaf

2 tablespoons extra-virgin olive oil

1 teaspoon English mustard

a few drops of Tabasco sauce

500 g (1 lb 2 oz) unpasteurised fresh white crabmeat

2 hard-boiled eggs, shelled and roughly chopped

3 tablespoons fresh mayonnaise

2 ripe vine tomatoes, sliced

shredded iceberg lettuce

salt and freshly ground white pepper

A special sandwich indeed! Although crabmeat is available all year round, the best season to buy it is from April to December. If you plan to buy fresh crabs and prepare them yourself, make sure you ask for a cock crab as he contains more white meat. However, if that seems daunting, you can buy fresh unpasteurised white crabmeat that has an excellent flavour at the fishmonger.

1 Heat a large griddle pan or plate on the hob and cook the bacon rashers for 2–3 minutes, until crispy. Or cook under a preheated grill. Remove and keep warm.

2 Cut three slices lengthways from the bloomer loaf about 2.5 cm (1 in) thick. Brush with a little olive oil, arrange on the hot grill plate or under the grill and cook for 1–2 minutes on each side until toasted and charred with lines.

3 Stir the mustard, Tabasco, crabmeat and hard-boiled eggs into the mayonnaise. Season to taste.

4 Arrange the tomatoes on the first slice of bread, followed by the bacon and then half the crabmeat mixture. Spread another slice of bread with the remaining crabmeat mixture and stack on top of the first slice of bread. Scatter over some shredded lettuce to cover. Finish with the last slice of bread and secure with small wooden kebab skewers or cocktail sticks. Cut into chunky sandwiches and serve at once.

CHEF'S TIP
Don't throw away any leftover bread – blitz in a food processor to fine breadcrumbs and freeze – the crumbs keep in the freezer for 2 months and are bound to come in handy. They can be used from frozen.

2 thin flatbreads or flour tortillas

25 g (1 oz) Jarlsberg or other hard cheese such as Cheddar, thinly sliced

1 slice of Parma ham

a few fresh basil leaves

1–2 teaspoons sweet chilli sauce

Silvana's
CHILLI CHEESE TORTILLA SANDWICH

Incredibly easy and packed with flavour, this was created as perfect post-pub food. It can be stacked higher to accommodate however many people you are feeding and requires very little by way of skill. Ben was doubtful that the flavour of Parma ham and sweet chilli sauce was a tasty combination but it proved a winner.

1 Heat a large, non-stick frying pan.

2 Place one flatbread or flour tortilla in the hot pan and arrange the cheese on top. Tear over the Parma ham and basil leaves and then drizzle over some sweet chilli sauce, top with the remaining bread and cook for a further minute or so until the underside is crisp and flecked with brown spots.

3 Turn the sandwich and cook for a further 1 minute. Cut into wedges, fold a paper napkin round and eat hot.

CHEF'S TIP

If you are feeding more than one person, once you have turned the sandwich, scatter over more of the filling followed by another flatbread, before turning and cooking for an extra minute. Continue to layer in the same way, but take care as you turn over the stack.

Ben's
THAI HOT AND SOUR SOUP

SERVES 4

1–2 red chillies, chopped

2 teaspoons palm sugar

1 stick of lemongrass, tough outer layers removed, sliced

3–4 coriander roots

juice of 3 limes

2 tablespoons Thai fish sauce (nam pla)

1.2 litres (2 pints) fresh chicken stock

12 cleaned raw king prawns

8 shiitake mushrooms, sliced

soy sauce

This soup is a flavour explosion. It's clear in style, simple, very quick to make and versatile too. Put in it whatever you like, but I like prawns and shiitake mushrooms.

1 Pound together the chillies, palm sugar, lemongrass and coriander roots in a mortar and pestle to a coarse paste. Add the lime juice and fish sauce and pound until well combined. Alternatively, lightly blitz in a food processor.

2 Bring the stock to the boil in a large saucepan. Add the prawns, shiitake mushrooms and enough of the spice mixture until the required taste is achieved. (I like to add it all but you might find it better to start by adding half and then tasting and adding more to suit your own palate.) Cook for 3–4 minutes. Serve immediately, with soy sauce to taste.

50 g (2 oz) butter

4 shallots, roughly chopped

2 garlic cloves, crushed

1 large potato, weighing about 350 g (12 oz), peeled and diced into 1 cm (1/2 in) cubes

750 g (1 lb 10 oz) small white closed cup button mushrooms

2 teaspoons plain white flour

1.2 litres (2 pints) hot chicken stock, fresh or from a cube

150 ml (5 fl oz) double cream

5 bunches of watercress, about 350 g (12 oz), very ends chopped off

salt and freshly ground black pepper

Paul's

WATERCRESS AND MUSHROOM SOUP

A classic velouté (smooth, velvety and creamy) style soup. Good ingredients are the key here and don't add that watercress too early. I like to finish mine with a drop of white truffle oil – an indulgence, but worth it.

1 Melt the butter in a large saucepan and gently fry the shallots and garlic over a low heat for 6–8 minutes, until softened but not browned.

2 Add the potato and button mushrooms and dust with the flour. Pour over the chicken stock and stir well to prevent any lumps. Bring to the boil and simmer for 6–8 minutes or until the potatoes are just tender.

3 Stir in the double cream and bring back to just under the boil. Stir in the watercress, allowing it to wilt slightly and then immediately remove from the heat.

4 Purée in batches in a food processor. Pass through a sieve into a clean pan and reheat gently to serve hot, or pour into a clean bowl and chill quickly to retain all that wonderful colour if keeping aside to serve later. Check the seasoning before serving.

CHEF'S TIP
In the restaurant, we serve this soup in cappuccino cups with a frothy top – simply pop a milk frother (such as an aerolatte) into the soup and whizz until frothy.

SERVES 4

750 ml (generous 1¼ pints) milk

2 garlic cloves

a bunch of spring onions

1 teaspoon cumin seeds

1 teaspoon ground turmeric

1 large cauliflower

2 tablespoons olive oil

2 tablespoons grated Parmesan cheese

½ small ciabatta loaf

100 g (4 oz) pancetta, cubed

salt and freshly ground black pepper

Silvana's
VELVET CAULIFLOWER SOUP

This lovely, super-smooth soup with its crunchy, cheesy croûtons is a great all-rounder. Make it during the summer months when cauliflower is in abundance or in the winter as a warming, hearty supper.

1 Preheat the oven to 200°C/400°F/Gas Mark 6. Pour the milk into a large pan and place on the heat. Roughly chop the garlic and the white part of the spring onions and add to the pan. Set aside the green spring onion ends. Stir in the cumin seeds and turmeric.

2 Cut off and discard the outer green leaves from the cauliflower. Cut the cauliflower into small florets and add to the milk pan, with some salt. Bring to the boil then lower the heat, partially cover and simmer for 20 minutes until the cauliflower is completely tender.

3 Meanwhile, place the oil in a large bowl and add the Parmesan and a good grinding of black pepper. Cut the bread into roughly 2 cm (¾ in) cubes. Add to the bowl, toss well and then spread out on a non-stick baking sheet, ensuring they lie in a single layer. Bake for 15–20 minutes, until crunchy and golden brown.

4 Empty the pancetta cubes into a non-stick frying pan and cook over a medium heat for 5 minutes or so, stirring from time to time, until crisp and golden. Drain on kitchen paper.

5 Finely slice the reserved spring onion greens.

6 Blend the soup in a liquidizer until velvety-smooth; alternatively, blitz with a hand-blender and then pass through a fine sieve. Check the seasoning and then ladle into bowls. Scatter over the crunchy croûtons, crispy pancetta and green onions. Serve at once.

3 BEST · SPICE TIPS

BEN Always use spices in the whole state. I buy them and store them in cigar boxes to keep them fresh. I do my own grinding every time I need them. Coriander and nutmeg are especially useful: great all-round spices.

PAUL I never buy ground spices. Always use whole spices and dry-fry them – this creates different flavour blends. You can actually create a separate spice. One of my favourite blends is roasted cumin and coriander, properly called dhana jeera, a fantastic spice to rub into meats before grilling.

SILVANA I buy ground spices but always shop around for them from the most authentic source. I always buy my paprika from the Spanish deli, my cardamom from an Indian store and chillies from the Italian deli. I always put a few dried chillies in my peppercorn grinder for an extra kick.

Ben's
FOUR-CHEESE FONDUE

SERVES 4

1 garlic clove, halved

5 g dried porcini, soaked in hot water and minced

300 ml (10 fl oz) German Riesling or Spätlese white wine

juice of ¹/₂ lemon

250 g (9 oz) Comté cheese, grated

250 g (9 oz) Gruyère cheese, grated

250 g (9 oz) Emmental cheese, grated

250 g (9 oz) Reblochon cheese, chopped

2 teaspoons Calvados

salt and freshly ground white pepper

To serve:

200 g (7 oz) honey-roast ham, cut into large cubes

200 g (7 oz) fresh pineapple, cut into large cubes

200 g (7 oz) focaccia, toasted, cut into large cubes

olive oil, to drizzle

Fondue is one of those things that you either love or hate. It's a real step back in time. You can't beat dunking toasty bread or some lovely ham or fruit into the luscious creamy, stringy, melted cheese. Fondue is a great party pleaser, so get the fondue pot out and have a crack.

1 Rub the inside of a fondue pan or large, heavy-based saucepan with the cut side of the halved clove of garlic, then discard the garlic.

2 Put the pan on to a moderate heat, add the minced porcini, white wine and lemon juice and warm through.

3 Stir in the cheeses and heat gently until melted. Do not allow to boil.

4 Add the Calvados and simmer until thickened. Season to taste with white pepper (you may not need any salt because the cheese is quite salty). Keep hot and serve with the chunky cubes of ham, pineapple and toasted focaccia, drizzled with olive oil and seasoned.

SERVES 6 (MAKES ABOUT 36 BEIGNETS)

60 g (2¹/₄ oz) butter

120 g (4¹/₂ oz) plain white flour, sifted

3 eggs, lightly beaten

50 g (2 oz) dried chorizo, finely chopped

25 g (1 oz) Parmesan cheese, finely grated

2 teaspoons chopped fresh tarragon

4 tablespoons sweetcorn kernels

100 g (4 oz) cooked new potatoes, skinned and crushed

50 g (2 oz) Roquefort cheese

oil for deep-frying

Paul's

PARTY CHEESE BEIGNETS

These are great as canapés or as a cunning addition to a salad. It all starts with a basic choux paste and from there all options are open. I've used crushed new potatoes, Roquefort, Parmesan and chorizo to flavour these light golden puffs – ring the changes and experiment with a few of your favourite ingredients but, beware, the beignets are very moreish!

1 Put 150 ml (5 fl oz) water into a heavy-based saucepan. Add the butter and bring slowly to the boil (by the time the water boils, the butter should be completely melted).

2 When the mixture is boiling, add all the flour in one go. Beat the mixture hard with a wooden spoon until well combined. Cook for about 1 minute, stirring constantly, until the mixture is thick, smooth and leaves the sides of the pan. Allow to cool slightly.

3 Beat in the eggs, a little at a time, until the mixture is soft, shiny and smooth.

4 Divide the mixture into two different bowls. Stir the chorizo, Parmesan cheese, tarragon and sweetcorn into one mixture until just combined. Stir the new potatoes and the Roquefort into the second until all are just combined.

5 Half-fill a deep saucepan with oil. Just before serving, bring the oil to 180°C/350°F. If you do not have a thermometer, drop a cube of bread into the oil: it should sizzle and turn brown in 45 seconds. Drop teaspoonfuls of the choux mixture into the oil (you'll be able to cook about a dozen at a time) and cook for 1–2 minutes until golden brown. Drain on kitchen paper and keep warm while cooking the remaining mixture. Serve immediately.

Silvana's

GOATS' CHEESE & CRANBERRY TOAST

SERVES 1

1 thick slice of sourdough bread

1–2 teaspoons cranberry or redcurrant jelly

100 g (4 oz) disc of chèvre (goats' cheese)

about 1 tablespoon extra-virgin olive oil

a handful of wild rocket leaves

balsamic vinegar

salt and freshly ground black pepper

Not just any old cheese on toast – this is a marvellous blend of creamy cheese and sweet cranberry or red-currant jelly topped with the peppery fresh flavour of rocket, all on a base of crunchy toasted sourdough bread. Scrumptious.

1 Toast the bread on one side under a medium grill. Roughly spread the cranberry or redcurrant jelly on the untoasted side of the bread and sit the cheese on top. Drizzle over some olive oil and season with salt and pepper.

2 Return to the grill for 3–4 minutes, until the cheese is golden and beginning to melt. Top with a handful of rocket leaves and a splash of balsamic vinegar and olive oil. Serve immediately.

SERVES 4

2 tablespoons roughly chopped fresh, wild (if possible) oregano

600 g (1 lb 5 oz) piece fresh tuna fillet (or belly)

100–150 ml (3½–5 fl oz) olive oil

1 garlic clove, thinly sliced

4 tablespoons dry white wine

salt and freshly ground black pepper

For the salad:

700 g (1 lb 9 oz) baby Jersey Royal new potatoes

celery leaves from firm, leafy celery, white inner leaves only

a small handful of fresh flatleaf parsley

2 tablespoons small capers, in salt or vinegar, drained

Ben's

BRAISED TUNA SALAD

I love tuna and eat it in many ways but this is my fave. It's a salad that has everything – juicy tuna, lovely rich dressing and a mouthwatering potato salad and it makes a great summertime lunch when tuna is at its best.

1 Preheat the oven to 180°C/350°F/Gas Mark 4.

2 Scatter the oregano and seasoning on to a plate and roll the tuna in it to coat evenly. Heat the olive oil over a low heat (it should be about 2.5 cm (1 in) deep) in a small pan and quickly seal the tuna on all sides (do not brown). Then add the garlic and white wine. Cover and place in oven for 3–4 minutes, depending on thickness. Remove and allow to rest. If tuna is thin, don't put it in the oven, just leave on top of stove.

3 Cook the potatoes in lightly salted, boiling water for 6–7 minutes, until tender. Drain and refresh in cold water. Drain again.

4 Meanwhile, boil the eggs for 3–4 minutes. Remove with a slotted spoon and run under cold water. When cold enough to handle, remove the shells, put the eggs in a large bowl and mash slightly with a fork. Stir in the mustard, anchovies, white-wine vinegar and Parmesan. Whisk in the olive oil, until emulsified. The dressing should be thick enough to coat a spoon.

5 Fold the dressing into the potatoes, celery, parsley and capers to coat evenly (reserving a few celery leaves for a garnish). Flake the tuna and carefully fold it into the potatoes, trying to prevent it from flaking any further. Serve scattered with the reserved celery leaves.

For the dressing:

2 eggs

1 tablespoon Dijon mustard

3 anchovy fillets, chopped

1 tablespoon white-wine vinegar

50 g (2 oz) Parmesan cheese, grated finely

150 ml (5 fl oz) extra-virgin olive oil

Paul's RARE PEPPERED TUNA

SERVES 4

600 g (1 lb 5 oz) tuna loin

4–5 teaspoons finely cracked black peppercorns

For the dressing:

¼ teaspoon wasabi paste (Japanese horseradish)

finely grated rind and juice of 1 lime

1 tablespoon chopped fresh coriander

½ small red onion, finely chopped

3 tablespoons extra-virgin olive oil

1 tablespoon sweet chilli sauce

For the Asian coleslaw:

1 small carrot, cut into fine matchsticks

1 small red onion, finely sliced

1 tablespoon chopped fresh coriander

4 tablespoons shredded Chinese leaf

1 nashi/Asian pear or crisp green apple, quartered, cored and thinly sliced

2.5 cm (1 in) piece of fresh root ginger, cut into thin matchsticks

2 tablespoons chopped fresh mint

50 g (2 oz) beansprouts

The current trend for Japanese food has meant that most supermarkets now stock fresh tuna. But if you want really fresh tuna, pre-order it from a fishmonger and ask for a square piece of tuna loin about 15 cm (6 in) long and about 5 cm (2 in) square. I like the rare-cooked aspect of this dish and the coleslaw is an ideal accompaniment, not forgetting the kick from the wasabi and lime dressing.

1 Roll the tuna in the cracked black pepper and sear on all sides in a very hot frying pan. This will only take a couple of minutes (only the very outside of the tuna should be cooked). Cover and chill until ready to use.

2 Mix the dressing ingredients together. Season to taste and then toss with the coleslaw ingredients. Check the seasoning again.

3 Slice the tuna into 5 mm (¼ in) thick slices and arrange on individual serving plates with a spoonful of the salad. Serve at once.

CHEF'S TIP

If you haven't tried wasabi, then you are in for a real treat – it's Japanese horseradish, a bright green and hot condiment. Fresh wasabi is hard to come by, but powdered wasabi, to which you add water to make a paste, or ready-made pastes in a tube, can be found in some large supermarkets. If not, a trip to your local Japanese deli is necessary. Watch out: a little goes a very long way!

SERVES 4

400 g (14 oz) fresh skinless, boneless tuna or salmon

6 spring onions

a handful of fresh coriander leaves, plus a few sprigs, to garnish

2 teaspoons horseradish sauce

sunflower oil, for shallow-frying

2 tablespoons plain white flour

salt and freshly ground black pepper

To serve:

4 crusty bread rolls

2 Little Gem lettuce hearts

1 tomato

1 mini cucumber

a small jar of mayonnaise

1 lime

Silvana's

TUNA AND HORSERADISH BURGER

Everybody loves a burger and these are really easy to make and offer a healthier alternative to traditional beef burgers. Oily fish such as tuna and salmon make fantastic burgers, as they don't dry out during cooking. The horseradish gives a gentle kick and the coriander adds a lovely fresh flavour.

1 Cut the fish into large chunks, place in a food processor and pulse until roughly minced. Transfer to a bowl.

2 Thinly slice the spring onions and add to the mince, with the coriander leaves, horseradish sauce and lots of salt and pepper. Using damp hands, shape the mixture into four even-sized patties.

3 Heat a little oil in a large, non-stick frying pan. Dust the burgers in the flour, shaking off any excess. Shallow-fry for 3–4 minutes on each side until just cooked through. Drain on kitchen paper.

4 Split open the buns, slice the lettuce, tomato and cucumber and scatter over the base of the buns. Top each with a burger and dollop of mayo. Replace the lids and serve each with a wedge of lime for squeezing over.

Ben's
LOVAGE STEAMED MONKFISH

SERVES 2

1 large bunch of lovage or celery
leaves

100 g (4 oz) Maldon sea salt

400 g (14 oz) skinned fillet of monk-
fish tail

1 dried chilli, crushed

finely grated zest and 1/2 juice of
1 orange

6 organic carrots, peeled and cut
into chunks

2 tablespoons olive oil

a pinch of ground cumin

a pinch of ground cinnamon

1/2 small bunch of coriander leaves,
picked and stored in iced water
in fridge

1 small bulb of fennel, finely
sliced and stored in iced water
in fridge

juice of 1/2 lemon

salt and freshly ground black pepper

Monkfish is one of my favourite fish, and with its meaty, firm texture and subtle taste it is always a winner, even though the judges thought otherwise (what do they know?)! Gently steamed, it's perfect, and the combination of these classic North-African flavours really puts it in the best category.

1 Preheat the oven to the lowest setting possible. Cover a baking sheet with a piece of baking parchment. Pound the lovage or celery leaves and salt together in a pestle and mortar and sprinkle evenly over the paper. Bake for 1–2 hours, until dried out.

2 Slice the monkfish into six rounds about 4 cm (1½ in) thick. Chill until ready to use. Then, using a knife, make criss-cross cuts (about 1 cm (½ in) deep) across the surface of the fish round. Season with the lovage salt, dried chilli and orange zest.

3 Toss the carrots with 1 tablespoon of the olive oil, season with salt and freshly ground black pepper and put into a steamer or steamer basket set over a pan of boiling water. Steam for 8–10 minutes until very tender. Transfer to a food processor and purée until smooth. Pass through a sieve. Check the seasoning and add the cumin, cinnamon and a squeeze of the orange juice. Keep warm.

4 Lay the seasoned rounds on the steamer for 2–3 minutes until cooked through.

5 Meanwhile, drain the coriander and fennel and pat dry with kitchen paper. Whisk together the remaining olive oil and the lemon juice and season with salt and freshly ground black pepper. Toss with the fennel and coriander.

6 To serve, spoon the carrot purée around each serving plate. Arrange the steamed monk-fish, seasoned-side upwards, around the edge of the plate and place a pile of the salad in the centre. Serve at once.

Paul's

ROAST HAKE AND PANCETTA

Full of big Spanish flavours, this dish will always impress. Hake is under-used in Britain but the Spanish love it. Its flesh is milky-white and delicate in flavour. Fillets or cutlets are fragile – handle with care during cooking to prevent them from breaking up. Be brave: cut the squid, wrap the hake, steam the mussels and unleash the flavours. If you want to prepare ahead, make the broth up to the end of step 3 the previous day and keep in the fridge to reheat when needed.

1 To clean the mussels, scrub them well and scrape off any barnacles. Remove any 'beards' poking out from between the shells. Discard any that do not close when tapped on the work surface. Wrap each piece of fish in two slices of pancetta. Cover and chill until ready to use.

2 Put the cleaned mussels in a hot pan and pour over the boiling stock. Bring back to the boil and cook for 3–4 minutes, until the mussels are all open. Discard any that do not open. Strain, reserving the stock. Remove the mussels from their shells, cut in half and set aside.

3 Heat 1 tablespoon of the oil in a large, shallow pan and fry the squid and garlic over a high heat for 30 seconds to 1 minute. Add the white wine and saffron, bring to the boil and reduce by a third. Add the reserved mussel stock and simmer, uncovered, for 30 minutes to 1 hour until reduced by about one third again.

4 Heat the remaining oil in a frying pan and fry the hake fillets for 3–4 minutes, turning once.

5 Add the mussels, flatleaf parsley, capers and tomatoes to the squid, garlic and stock mixture. Remove from the heat, stir in the butter to lightly enrichen the stock and season to taste.

6 Wilt the spinach in a wok and season.

7 To serve, divide the mussels and squid mixture between four shallow serving bowls, arrange the spinach over the top and then the fish. Serve immediately.

SERVES 4

1 kg (2 lb 4 oz) live mussels

4 pieces of hake fillet, skin-on, weighing about 175–225 g (6–8 oz)

8 thin slices of pancetta

600 ml (1 pint) hot chicken stock

2 tablespoons olive oil

16 baby squid tubes, cleaned and cut into rings

1 garlic clove, finely chopped

100 ml (3½ fl oz) white wine

a pinch of saffron

1 tablespoon chopped fresh flatleaf parsley

1 tablespoon fine capers in brine

2 plum tomatoes, skinned, seeded and diced

a knob of unsalted butter

500 g (1 lb 2 oz) baby spinach

salt and freshly ground black pepper

Silvana's

HADDOCK AND MUSHY PEA FISHCAKES

In my home town of Derby, mushy peas are really popular, especially on a trip to the chippy. Now that I'm based in London, where people, namely my husband, most definitely turn their nose up at the very thought of mushy peas, I do miss having them on the side of my plate. However, I have found that incorporating them into the dish like these fishcakes, means I get to eat them and no one's any the wiser. And they also got top marks from *The Best's* tasters.

SERVES 4

700 g (1 lb 9 oz) floury potatoes, e.g. Maris Piper or King Edward, peeled and diced

400 g (14 oz) haddock fillet

300 ml (10 fl oz) milk

1 tablespoon mint jelly

300 g can of mushy peas

2 tablespoons plain white flour, seasoned

1 egg, beaten

8–10 tablespoons natural dried breadcrumbs

sunflower oil, for frying

1 lemon

3 tablespoons mayonnaise

coarse sea salt and freshly ground black pepper

For the chunky chips:

3 large red potatoes, e.g. Desirée

1–2 tablespoons olive oil

1 Preheat the oven to 220°C/425°F/Gas Mark 7. Cook the diced potatoes in a large pan of boiling water for 12–15 minutes, until tender.

2 Cut the red skins into chunky chips and cook in a separate pan of boiling water for 5 minutes. Pour the olive oil into a shallow baking tray and place in the oven.

3 Place the haddock in a sauté pan and pour over the milk. Cover, bring to the boil and then remove from the heat and set aside for 5 minutes or so, until cooked through.

4 Drain the chunky chips in a colander, shaking them well to roughen-up the edges a little. Remove the hot tray from the oven and tip in the chips, tossing to coat them in the hot oil. Sprinkle with salt and return to the oven for 15–20 minutes, until crisp and golden brown.

5 Drain the diced potatoes well and return to the pan. Add the mint jelly and some salt and pepper and mash together. Remove the fish from the pan and drain it well, discarding the milk. Flake the fish into the potatoes. Add the mushy peas and stir together. Shape the mixture into four firm, even-sized cakes.

6 Dust the cases lightly with seasoned flour. Put the beaten egg in a shallow bowl and spread out the breadcrumbs on a plate. Then dip the fishcakes into the beaten egg and then into the breadcrumbs.

7 Heat a little sunflower oil in a frying pan and gently cook the fishcakes for 2 minutes on each side until crisp and golden. Drain on kitchen paper. The fishcakes may have to be cooked in two batches.

8 Cut the lemon into wedges. Squeeze a little lemon juice into the mayonnaise. Divide the fishcakes and chips between two plates and serve each with a dollop of lemon mayo and a lemon wedge.

48

SERVES 4

1 kg (2 lb 4 oz) live mussels

1 can of a lager of your choice, e.g. Victoria Bitter

400 g can of plum tomatoes, drained and roughly chopped

1 red chilli, finely chopped

3 garlic cloves, roughly chopped

2 tablespoons olive oil

1 bunch of spring onions, trimmed green ends only

crusty French bread, to serve

Ben's

BARBECUED BEER AND CHILLI MUSSELS

When it comes to barbecues, the Aussies know the score. And who else would have thought to barbecue mussels? But it works really well; all you need is a flat iron barbecue plate, a hot day, some beer and a bunch of mates.

1 To clean the mussels, scrub the shells and scrape off any barnacles. Pull out any 'beards' that protrude from between the shells and discard any that do not close when tapped on the work surface.

2 Preheat a flat griddle plate on top of the hot coals of a barbecue until smoking. Pour over a little beer and wait until the beer has evaporated.

3 Throw on the mussels, then the tomatoes, chilli and garlic. With a scraper or barbecue fish slice, move the mussels around the grill plate. Pour over just enough beer to cover the base of the grill plate (you won't need to use the whole can) and drizzle over the olive oil.

4 Place a large heatproof bowl over the mussels to allow them to steam and open. Discard any that do not open. Toss in the spring onion tops and serve with a can of beer and the French bread.

50

Paul's
BARBECUED SNAPPER AND CITRUS BROTH

Well, Ben may be the barbecue king, but this dish seems to work well over the coals. It's the sauce that really lifts the dish. It's an exciting, fast stir-fry that will teach your tastebuds to pick out the flavours. Mark Miller's Coyote Café in Santa Fe is a chilli-lover's delight, and this recipe is loosely based on an idea of his.

THE BEST **SEAFOOD BARBECUE** THE BEST **SEAFOOD BARBECUE** THE BEST **SEAFOOD BARBECUE** THE

SERVES 4

1 fennel bulb, very thinly sliced

1 banana shallot, peeled and sliced

a small bunch of fresh chives or chervil, chopped

sea salt

1 kg (2 lb 4 oz) red snapper, cleaned

1 tablespoon olive oil

For the broth:

1 tablespoon olive oil

2 red and 2 yellow peppers, seeded, cored and cut into fine matchsticks

2 green and 2 red chillies, seeded and thinly sliced

2 garlic cloves, chopped

5 cm (2 in) piece of fresh root ginger, peeled and cut into fine matchsticks

1.2 litres (2 pints) light chicken stock, fresh or from a cube

finely grated zest and juice of 1 orange

finely grated zest and juice of 1 lemon

finely grated zest and juice of 1 lime

1 tablespoon caster sugar

2 tablespoons chopped fresh coriander

salt and freshly ground black pepper

1 Toss together the fennel, shallot and chives or chervil, season with sea salt and freshly ground black pepper and use to stuff the belly of the snapper.

2 Prepare the barbecue. Rub the tablespoon of olive oil over the snapper and barbecue over medium-hot coals for 15–20 minutes, turning carefully only once.

3 Meanwhile, make the broth. Heat the oil in a large wok or frying pan. Add the peppers, chillies, garlic and ginger and cook over a high heat, stirring occasionally, for 5–8 minutes, until softened. Stir in the stock. Add the citrus zest and juices to taste (you may not want to use it all) and the sugar. Bring to the boil and simmer for 10 minutes. Stir in the coriander and season to taste.

4 Place the snapper in a shallow serving bowl and ladle over the stock and vegetables. If you prefer to, you can carefully remove the fillets from the snapper before serving.

SERVES 2

1 small bunch of mint

3 spring onions, roughly chopped

1 garlic clove, roughly chopped

1 Scotch Bonnet chilli, roughly chopped

a small bunch of fresh flatleaf parsley

2 tablespoons olive oil

6 cleaned sardines, weighing about 50–85 g (2–3 oz) each

1 large orange

sea salt and freshly ground black pepper

Silvana's
ORANGE BARBECUED SARDINES

Sardines on the barbecue always herald the onset of summer in my garden. The herbs in the cavity add both flavour and fragrance to the fish. These can be cooked under a hot grill, should it, by any chance, rain.

1 Prepare the barbecue or preheat the grill to medium-high.

2 Strip the leaves from the mint, discarding the stems. Mix the roughly chopped spring onions, garlic and chilli together on a chopping board and chop finely using a heavy knife. Then add the herbs and roughly chop those into the mixture too. Add a large pinch of coarse salt and a good grind of black pepper. Drizzle a tablespoon of olive oil over the top and mix together.

3 Spoon the herb mixture into the sardine cavities. Thinly slice the orange and wrap one slice round each sardine, to cover the cavity and enclose the filling. Tie in place with a strong piece of string.

4 Rub the outside of the fish with a little more olive oil and season lightly. Barbecue or grill for 3–4 minutes on each side, until the skin is crisp and patched with brown. Transfer to plates and serve with a simple green salad.

Ben's CHINESE STEEPED CHICKEN

I love the aromas and spices used in Chinese cooking. They are often clean and simple and this dish is both of these – simple to make, subtly complex and very healthy. It's something I love to cook and eat all the time. And you kill two birds with one stone because you end up with an awesome stock you can use in other Asian soups and noodles dishes. So keep the stock in the freezer to use later on.

1 Rinse the inside of each poussin with the vinegar and discard the liquid.

2 Smash the lemongrass with a rolling pin and cut into two pieces. Put a piece into the cavity of each bird.

3 Place the poussin in a large pot and cover with water. Add half the ginger, 1 chilli, star anise, 2 cloves of garlic, peppercorns, lime leaves, half the spring onions and the soy sauce. Bring to the boil and add the salt. Simmer for 5 minutes, put the lid on and turn off heat. Allow to stand for 40 minutes.

4 Remove the poussins from the stock and drain. Bring the stock back to the boil and steam broccoli over the top in a colander or steamer for 3–4 minutes.

5 Meanwhile, chop the remaining chilli and place in a small bowl with enough soy sauce to cover the chilli, to form a dip.

6 Cut the poussins into portions and lay on a platter. Cut the remaining garlic, ginger and spring onions into fine matchsticks and sprinkle over the poussin. Pour over a ladleful of stock. Sprinkle with more vinegar, soy sauce and sesame oil and serve with the broccoli, tossed in the oyster sauce, and the chilli/soy dip.

SERVES 2

150 ml (5 fl oz) Chinese red vinegar or red-wine vinegar, plus extra to serve

2 poussins, weighing about 450 g (1 lb) each

1 lemongrass stem

2.5 cm (1 in) piece of fresh root ginger, peeled and thickly sliced

1 red chilli, pricked with a fork

1 star anise

4 garlic cloves, smashed

2 black peppercorns

2 lime leaves

1 bunch of spring onions, trimmed and cut in half

1 tablespoon dark soy sauce

$1/4$ teaspoon salt

To serve:

300 g (10 oz) Chinese sprouting broccoli

1 chilli, chopped

soy sauce

sesame oil

1–2 tablespoons oyster sauce

HERB TIPS

3 BEST

BEN I like to dry big bunches of the more robust herbs like rosemary and thyme so I can use them whenever I want. I make herb oils from fresh herbs. Bruise them in a pestle and mortar with some good olive oil and store in a bottle, ready for brushing on to meat, fish and vegetables.

PAUL I like freezing puréed garlic in ice-cube trays, ready for whenever I need it, whether it's a sauce, stir-fry or even rubbing straight on to meat. When chopping herbs, I never throw stalks away. The whole flavour of the herbs lies in their roots and so use them too for the best flavour.

SILVANA I do like growing my own herbs. If I ever have any spare of the soft ones like chervil and chives, I freeze them in ziplock bags and then crumble them into my cooking as I need them. If buying them from the supermarket, I buy freeze-dried ones. These are the best because the flavour is locked in.

SERVES 4

For the marinade:

150 ml (5 fl oz) natural yoghurt

2 tablespoons fresh lemon juice

1 tablespoon chopped garlic

1 tablespoon finely chopped fresh root ginger

2 long red chillies with seeds, roughly chopped

1/2 tablespoon chopped fresh mint

4 tablespoons roughly chopped coriander

1 teaspoon garam masala

1 teaspoon gram flour

1/2 tablespoon medium curry powder

1 teaspoon salt

1 teaspoon ground cumin

For the chicken:

4 organic or maize-fed skinless chicken breasts

1–2 tablespoons olive oil

For the dressing:

100 ml (3 1/2 fl oz) rice-wine vinegar

finely grated zest and juice of 2 limes

4 tablespoons caster sugar

2 red chillies, seeded and finely chopped

4 chapatis, to serve

Paul's

TANDOORI-STYLE CHICKEN

A big hit with the camera crew (more so than with the tasters, unfortunately), this is my version of a classic. Yoghurt is a wonderful base for a marinade, penetrating the meat and tenderizing it and forming a delicate crust around the meat during cooking, keeping it moist. (I'm still sore that Silvana's chicken wings beat this! Who chose those tasters?)

1 Place all the marinade ingredients together in a blender and blend until smooth. Transfer to a bowl. Alternatively, finely chop the garlic, ginger, chillies, mint and coriander and blend with the remaining marinade ingredients.

2 Slash the chicken breast in three or four places. Add the chicken to the marinade and turn to coat evenly. Cover and leave to marinate for 24 hours, if possible. Toss all the salad ingredients together and season to taste.

3 Lift the chicken out of the marinade. Heat the oil in a large frying pan until smoking and pan-fry the chicken for 12–15 minutes until slightly charred.

4 Whisk the rice vinegar, lime zest and juice, sugar and chillies together and toss with the salad ingredients. Serve immediately, with the chicken and a chapati.

For the salad:

1 small fresh pineapple, finely diced

100 g (4 oz) mooli (Japanese white radish), cut into thin matchsticks

250 g (9 oz) mangetout, cut length-ways into thin strips

2 carrots, cut into thin matchsticks

2 cm (³/₄ in) piece of fresh root ginger, peeled and cut into thin matchsticks

1 red onion, finely sliced

1 heaped tablespoon chopped fresh coriander

a handful of miso cress (optional)

Silvana's
SPICY FRIED CHICKEN WINGS

SERVES 4

12 large chicken wings

4 tablespoons plain white flour

3 teaspoons Cajun seasoning

2 teaspoons smoked paprika

1 teaspoon table salt

For the chutney:

1 large mango

1 shallot, finely chopped

3 tablespoons red-wine vinegar

3 tablespoons light brown sugar

1/4 teaspoon salt

1/2 teaspoon black mustard seeds

1 star anise

The very best dish for sharing. Unexpected friends on the doorstep? Football on TV? It'll take a matter of minutes to get a tray of wings in the oven. Serve with my quick chutney or stir some chopped red onion into a pot of yoghurt for an even quicker dip. The chutney also does very nicely in a Cheddar-cheese sandwich.

1 Preheat the oven to 200°C/400°F/Gas Mark 6. Using a strong pair of scissors, snip the tip off each wing.

2 In a large bowl, stir together the flour, Cajun seasoning, paprika and salt. Toss the wings in the seasoned flour and arrange on a wire rack. Place on a baking sheet and roast for 25–30 minutes, until crisp and golden brown.

3 To make the chutney, holding the mango firmly on a board, slice down either side of the central stone to remove the 'cheeks'. Using a large spoon, scoop out the flesh and discard the skin. Roughly dice the flesh and remove and dice any flesh still clinging to the stone.

4 Place in a pan with the shallot, vinegar, sugar, salt and spices. Cook over a medium heat for 15 minutes until most of the liquid has evaporated. Spoon into a serving bowl and serve with the chicken wings.

SERVES 4

4 two-finger-thick pork chops, cut from the rib-end of the loin

140 g (5 oz) butter

4 banana shallots, sliced lengthways

2 Granny Smith apples, each cut into eight wedges

2 tablespoons chopped fresh thyme

salt and freshly ground black pepper

Ben's

PORK CHOP IN A BAG

This one blows people away! The thing I love about it is the lovely way it's presented – a lovely pork chop, baked in a bag so it retains all its juices and with the apple and onion, it's amazing! For the best results I always choose well hung, organic Plantation, Gloucester Old Spot or Middle White pork for this recipe.

1 Cut the bone away from the meat, leaving just the round end attached, and scrape clean with a sharp knife. Season each chop with salt and pepper.

2 Preheat the oven to 200°C/400°F/Gas Mark 6. Cut four circles of baking parchment, each 40 cm (16 in) in diameter, large enough to wrap the pork chops.

3 Melt 25 g (1 oz) of the butter in a small frying pan and fry the chops on all sides for 1–2 minutes until golden brown.

4 Cut the remaining butter into eight equal-size pieces and place 1 piece of butter on each circle of paper. Over each circle, scatter some sliced shallots, four apple wedges, some of the thyme and salt and pepper. Place a pork chop on top and add another piece of butter and some more thyme. Wrap up the parcels, making sure they are well sealed. Secure with string around the bone. Bake for 20 minutes.

5 Cut the string, trim off the burnt paper and serve with mustard mashed potatoes or braised swiss chard.

3 BEST FLUFFY MASH TIPS

BEN The best fluffy mash would have to be from baked medium-sized potatoes, all the same size. Peel them while they're hot, push them through a potato ricer, add cold butter and then finish them off with double cream. Lovely.

PAUL For me, the best way of making mashed potatoes is not to let them sit in the boiled water; as soon as they're ready you've got to get them out. It's all about temperatures and starch, a little bit of hot milk and copious amounts of very, very cold unsalted butter beaten in with a wooden spoon. And I don't think you can beat that really.

SILVANA I think the trick is the mashing itself. I use a traditional masher. I don't mind the odd little lump and I'm not interested in sieving it and all of that kind of stuff. Mash it up, but when the potatoes are nearly ready, add hot milk and butter because I like them to be quite soft.

Paul's
PORK VINDALOO

SERVES 4

The spices:

1 star anise

2 tablespoons coriander seeds

2 tablespoons cumin seeds

6 cloves

2-inch cinnamon stick

2 teaspoons black peppercorns

2 teaspoons fenugreek seeds

2 teaspoons fennel seeds

For the marinade:

1/2 red pepper, seeded and roughly sliced

2 fresh tomatoes, quartered

6 red chillies, seeded and roughly chopped

50 ml (2 fl oz) red wine

50 ml (2 fl oz) red-wine vinegar

1 kg (2 lb 4 oz) lean pork from the leg or shoulder, cut into 5 cm (2 in) cubes

2 tablespoons vegetable oil

8 garlic cloves, chopped

1 onion, finely chopped

10–12.5 cm (4–5 in) piece of fresh root ginger, peeled and finely chopped

2 teaspoons soft dark brown sugar

200 g (7 oz) basmati rice

My culinary links with Zanzibar are via my mum who had many Indian friends when we lived on this exotic spice island. Through them she developed a real love of Indian food. This Goan, Portuguese-influenced, curry classic is hot and fiery but packed with so many flavours.

1 Dry-fry the spices in a heavy-based, non-stick pan until toasted. Allow to cool, then grind in a coffee grinder or mini blender. Alternatively, pound using a mortar and pestle.

2 Prepare the marinade by blending all the marinade ingredients together in a liquidizer.

3 Mix the spices into the blended marinade mixture and toss the pork through. Refrigerate and allow to marinate for as long as possible.

4 Heat 1 tablespoon of vegetable oil in a sauté pan and sauté the garlic, onion and ginger for a few minutes until softened and golden. Add the meat from the marinade and seal for 2 minutes. Add the marinade mixture and brown sugar and allow to cook on a low heat for 1 1/2 hours.

5 To cook the rice, heat the remaining tablespoon of vegetable oil in a pan and add the rice, leaving for 1 minute without stirring. Add enough water to cover the rice and then add another inch of water. Bring to the boil and simmer for 15 minutes. Cover the pan tightly with foil and place a tight-fitting lid on top. Leave to stand for a few minutes.

6 Fluff the rice up with a fork and serve with the vindaloo.

SERVES 4

1 kg (2 lb 4 oz) piece of belly pork

2 teaspoons Chinese five-spice powder

1 teaspoon smoked paprika

2 teaspoons salt

150 g (5½ oz) sushi rice (about 2 cupsfull)

4 teaspoons soy sauce

1 tablespoon vinegar

1 teaspoon Oriental chilli oil (check to make sure it contains shrimp paste)

1 tablespoon sesame seeds

2 tablespoons roughly chopped fresh coriander

CHINESE-STYLE BARBECUED PORK

I have made various versions of this for years, it truly is the best pork dish I can think of and makes an appearance on my dinnertable time and again. It's also excellent cooked on a barbecue.

1 Place the pork on a rack set over a roasting tin and pierce it in several places with a skewer. Pour over a kettle of boiling water and then pat dry with kitchen paper. Mix together the five-spice, paprika and salt and rub into the skin and flesh of the pork; set aside for up to 1 hour.

2 Preheat the oven to 220°C/425°F/Gas Mark 7. Drain the water out of the roasting tin, reposition the pork on a rack over the tin to catch any drips and then roast for 10 minutes. Lower the heat and cook for a further 30 minutes, until the pork is cooked through and the skin is crunchy.

3 Place the rice in a pan. Add 4 cups of water, bring to the boil, cover and cook for 15 minutes or so, until the rice is tender and the liquid has been absorbed.

4 In a shallow dish or baking sheet, mix together the soy sauce, vinegar and chilli oil. Add the cooked pork, crackling-side up, and leave to rest for a few minutes.

5 Toast the sesame seeds in a small non-stick pan and then stir into the rice, with the coriander. Spoon the rice on to serving plates. Slice the pork and arrange alongside the rice. Drizzle over the juices from the dish or baking sheet and serve.

CHEF'S TIP
A good alternative or addition to the sesame seeds is pickled ginger. Simply chop it and stir it through the rice.

Ben's
CRUNCHY POLENTA SHEPHERD'S PIE

SERVES 4–6

2 tablespoons olive oil

2 carrots, diced

3 celery sticks, diced

1 onion, diced

1 leek, white only, diced

1 turnip, diced

1 potato, weighing about 225 g (8 oz), peeled and diced

3 garlic cloves, finely chopped

500 g (1 lb 2 oz) leftover cooked lamb (meat taken from a leftover small roasted leg of lamb, cooked with rosemary and garlic works well), diced

a few black peppercorns

1 tablespoon yeast extract (I use Vegemite as it has a unique flavour)

1 vegetable stock cube, crumbled

For the polenta crust:

225 g (8 oz) fine instant polenta

100 ml (3$\frac{1}{2}$ fl oz) olive oil plus extra for oiling

100 g (4 oz) Parmesan cheese, finely grated

4 ripe tomatoes, sliced

salt and freshly ground black pepper

Straight away I thought of Grandma's shepherd's pie, but I wanted to jazz it up and give it a good crunchy top. She's 10,000 miles away, so I gave her a call. She said it could work: out came the crunchy polenta and, man, does it work! The judges said no, but I haven't heard from Grandma yet.

1 Heat the olive oil in a large pan and sauté all the vegetables until golden brown. Add the lamb, peppercorns, yeast extract, crumbled stock cube and enough water just to cover. Bring to the boil and simmer for about 45 minutes, until reduced and thickened. Season to taste.

2 Meanwhile, bring 1 litre (1$\frac{3}{4}$ pints) of lightly salted water to a rolling boil in a heavy-based saucepan. Whisk in the polenta in a continuous stream. Simmer for 3–4 minutes until cooked, stirring constantly. Remove from the heat and beat in the olive oil and Parmesan (reserving a little for the topping). Pour into a lightly oiled 23 x 33 cm (9 x 13 in) baking tray. Allow to cool and set.

3 Preheat the oven to 200°C/400°F/Gas Mark 6. Spoon the mince into a 1.7-litre (3-pint) ovenproof dish. Using a plain 6 cm (2$\frac{1}{2}$ in) cutter or an upturned glass, cut out circles from the polenta. Arrange the polenta circles alternately with the tomatoes on top of the mince, until completely covered. Sprinkle with the reserved Parmesan and bake for 30–40 minutes, or until golden brown and bubbling.

SERVES 8

For the stuffing:

2 tablespoons olive oil

1 small onion, finely chopped

2 teaspoons fresh thyme leaves

1 garlic clove, finely chopped

200 g (7 oz) mixed wild and cultivated mushrooms, e.g. oyster, small button, ceps, cleaned and quartered

1 chicken breast, weighing about 85–100 g (3–4 oz), cubed

1 small egg

300 g (10 oz) lamb trimmings, minced

2 tablespoons roughly chopped fresh flatleaf parsley

100 g (4 oz) chorizo or similar spicy sausage, skinned and finely diced

salt and freshly ground black pepper

For the saddle of lamb:

1 short saddle of lamb (excluding the chump) to serve 8 people, bone removed and the two fillets that sit on top of the bone detached

8 slices of unsmoked streaky bacon, rind removed

1 tablespoon vegetable oil

STUFFED LAMB SADDLE

The ultimate celebration roast. Ask your butcher to do all the hard work for you – boning out the saddle of lamb and detaching the two fillets. Then well-flavoured stuffing is all that is needed to produce this handsome roast (which won the points for me!). I use a meat probe to check that my roast is cooked. They're cheap to buy and a great investment if you're looking for perfection every time.

1 Preheat the oven to 180°C/350°F/Gas Mark 4. First, make the stuffing. Heat 1 tablespoon of the oil in a frying pan and sauté the onion, thyme leaves and garlic until soft. Turn on to a tray and leave to cool.

2 Add the remaining tablespoon of oil to the frying pan and fry the mushrooms for 2–3 minutes, until softened. Turn on to a tray and leave until cool enough to handle then roughly chop.

3 Place the chicken breast and egg in a food processor and process to a smooth paste. Add the minced lamb trimmings and continue to process for a few seconds more. Turn this mixture into a large bowl and add the onion mixture, mushrooms, parsley and chorizo. Season very well, as it needs to permeate the lamb.

To serve:

30 baby beetroot, washed and trimmed

a small bunch of fresh thyme

6 garlic cloves, smashed

2 tablespoons olive oil

gravy made with reduced red wine for a fuller flavour

4 Now stuff the lamb. Open out the saddle and spread the stuffing between the two loins. Use the handle of a wooden spoon to make two lengthways grooves. Lay the reserved lamb fillets in the grooves.

5 Roll the saddle up lengthways to enclose the stuffing. Cover each end with four strips of bacon and secure the saddle with string.

6 Heat the vegetable oil in a large frying pan and seal the saddle on all sides until golden brown. Roast in the middle of the oven. An average-sized saddle of lamb should take about 45–60 minutes to cook. If you have a meat probe, the centre temperature should be about 47°C/117°F.

7 Quickly prepare the beetroot for roasting. Place the prepared beetroot on a sheet of foil on a baking sheet. Season and scatter the thyme and garlic over. Drizzle with oil and scrunch the foil up to enclose in a parcel. Put the beetroot into the oven to roast straight away. Remove the lamb and beetroot from the oven after the cooking time and allow the meat to rest for 10 minutes before carving. Serve with a light red-wine gravy.

Silvana's

WARM LAMB SALAD

SERVES 4

2 garlic cloves

½ teaspoon ground cumin

500 g (1 lb 2 oz) boneless lamb, cubed

2 large aubergines, cubed

2 fresh rosemary sprigs

3–4 tablespoons olive oil

For the dressing:

1 small red onion, chopped

a small bunch of fresh mint, roughly chopped

a small bunch of fresh basil, roughly chopped

a small bunch of fresh flatleaf parsley, roughly chopped

juice of 2 limes

salt and freshly ground black pepper

warm bread, cherry tomatoes and a bowl of wild rocket leaves, to serve

Aubergine and lamb make one of the best flavour pairings I can think of. This is perfect for summer entertaining; give your mates a plate and a glass of chilled wine and let them help themselves.

1 Preheat the oven to 200°C/400°F/Gas Mark 6.

2 In a roasting tin, marinate the garlic, cumin, lamb and seasoning. Set aside for 10 minutes.

3 Add the aubergine, rosemary and half of the olive oil to the roasting tin. Roast for 30 minutes, stirring from time to time, until golden brown.

4 Meanwhile, make the dressing in a large bowl using the remaining olive oil, red onion, herbs, lime juice and seasoning.

5 Add the cooked mixture to the dressing and stir well. Allow the mixture to rest for 5 minutes before serving with the warm bread, tomatoes and wild rocket leaves.

SERVES 3

600 g (1 lb 5 oz) thick end of the fillet towards the back end of the loin (get the butcher to trim and tie it)

1 bunch of fresh thyme, leaves picked and chopped, stalks reserved

salt and freshly ground black pepper

extra-virgin olive oil

For the béarnaise sauce:

100 ml (3¹⁄₂ fl oz) malt vinegar

200 ml (7 fl oz) dry white wine

1 banana shallot, sliced

1 small bunch of fresh parsley, leaves chopped, stalks reserved

1 small bunch of fresh tarragon, leaves chopped, stalks reserved

1 teaspoon black peppercorns

500 g (1 lb 2 oz) unsalted butter

3 egg yolks

For the frites:

2 large King Edward potatoes, peeled and cut into equal-sized chips

Sunflower oil, for deep-frying

To serve:

1 head of broccoli, weighing about 250 g (9 oz), to serve

salt and freshly ground black pepper

extra-virgin olive oil

CHATEAUBRIAND STEAK AND FRITES

Roasted beef fillet, big fluffy chunky chips, beautifully tangy béarnaise sauce and my favourite steamed veg – broccoli. When it comes to the best beef, it has to be Châteaubriand, which is the thicker, more succulent end of the fillet.

1 Preheat the oven to 200°C/400°F/Gas Mark 6.

2 Roll the fillet in the thyme and some pepper. Tie up with string – wrap 2 or 3 loops around the fillet – to maintain its shape. Allow to rest at room temperature.

3 Meanwhile, make the béarnaise sauce. Put the malt vinegar, white wine, shallots, parsley stalks and some tarragon stalks and black peppercorns into a saucepan and simmer until the mixture is reduced by half. Strain. (Only half of this vinegar reduction will be used, so store the rest in the fridge to make a fantastic vinaigrette – or for a second batch of béarnaise.)

4 Microwave or heat the unsalted butter for 5 minutes, until it separates into a layer of buttermilk at the bottom, clear butterfat in the centre and a layer of foam at the top. Keep warm. This procedure is known as 'clarifying' the butter.

5 Sit a large glass bowl over a pan of simmering water and whisk together the egg yolks and half the vinegar reduction until it doubles in volume and leaves a trail.

6 Skim off the foam from the clarified butter, ladle the butter fat into the fluffy egg mixture and continue whisking until a thick consistency is reached and it coats the back of a spoon. If it becomes too thick, add a tablespoon of water. Add the chopped parsley and tarragon leaves and keep warm.

7 Boil the prepared potato frîtes for 4 minutes, until just cooked, and drain. Allow to cool.

8 Season the meat with salt and seal in a little heated olive oil in a heavy frying pan. Place on a bed of thyme stalks, and wack into the oven and cook for 15 minutes per pound. Allow to rest for 10 minutes before carving.

9 Just before serving, steam the broccoli with some salt and pepper and a drizzle of extra-virgin olive oil.

10 Heat the oil – when a cube of bread browns in 45 seconds, it's ready to fry – and deep-fry the frîtes. Slice the beef. Serve at once with the frîtes, steamed broccoli and béarnaise sauce.

Paul's

BRAISED RIB OF BEEF

OK, so Ben's Châteaubriand was fairly stunning, but this is real cooking! Rib trim – the meat between the ribs – is a little-seen cut of meat so ask your butcher to prepare this for you. Use a good-quality fresh stock and braise slowly, allowing the flavours to develop and enrich to the most heart-warming casserole ever! How did this not win points? If you're pushed for time, you can cook the beef and sauce and then store them overnight in the fridge, ready to add the finishing touches the next day.

SERVES 6

6 pieces of beef 'rib trim' or blade steak, weighing about 225 g (8 oz) each

2 tablespoons olive oil

1 carrot, diced

5 shallots, diced

1 celery stick, diced

$\frac{1}{2}$ head of garlic

a sprig of rosemary and thyme

a few black peppercorns

2 plum tomatoes, roughly chopped

350 ml (12 fl oz) red wine

1 litre (1$\frac{3}{4}$ pints) beef *jus* or fresh beef stock

1 tablespoon cornflour (optional)

2 tablespoons red wine (optional)

salt and freshly ground black pepper

For the garnish:

1 tablespoon vegetable oil

12 button onions

100 g (4 oz) pancetta, cut into lardons (short, thick strips)

140 g (5 oz) baby button mushrooms

50 g (2 oz) unsalted butter

12 cooked, peeled new potatoes

chopped fresh chervil

1 Season the beef with salt and pepper just before cooking. Heat the olive oil in a heavy-based casserole dish. Add the beef and fry in batches until the meat is browned on all sides to seal (this caramelises the natural sugars, giving the finished dish its wonderful rich colour). Remove with a slotted spoon and set aside. Pour away the excess oil.

2 Add the carrot, shallots and celery to the pan and cook for 2–3 minutes, stirring occasionally, until slightly browned and caramelised.

3 Stir in the garlic, rosemary, thyme, black peppercorns and tomatoes and cook for two minutes. Then add the red wine. Bring to the boil and simmer for 8–10 minutes, until reduced by half. Stir in the beef jus or fresh stock and return the pieces of beef to the pan. Cover and simmer very gently for 2 hours or until the meat is tender.

4 When the beef is cooked, transfer from the pan using a slotted spoon to a plate and keep warm. Pass the sauce through a sieve into a clean pan. Put the pan back on the heat. The sauce should be the consistency of double cream. If not, mix the cornflour with the red wine and gradually stir into the boiling sauce until the desired consistency is achieved. Return the meat to the pan. (This is an ideal stage to stop cooking, transfer the beef and sauce to a lidded container and store in the fridge until ready to use.)

5 Prepare the garnish. Heat the oil in a frying pan and sauté the onions and pancetta for 10 minutes, stirring occasionally, until golden brown and the onions are softened. Add the mushrooms and cook for a further 2 minutes. Melt the butter in a small frying pan and sauté the cooked potatoes until golden brown. Add the bacon, onions and mushrooms to the sauce and season to taste. Serve the beef scattered with the fresh chervil and the sautéed new potatoes.

SERVES 4

1 tablespoon olive oil

4 rashers of smoked streaky bacon

4 tablespoons plain white flour

750 g (1 lb 10 oz) casserole or braising steak, cubed

75 cl bottle of red wine

450 g jar silverskin pickled onions, drained and rinsed (250 g/9 oz drained weight)

3 tablespoons redcurrant jelly

2 fresh thyme sprigs

375 g pack of ready-rolled puff pastry

1–2 tablespoons of milk

salt and freshly ground black pepper

LAZY STEAK AND ONION PIE

I love a pickled onion and I was delighted how delicious they were when cooked into this hearty pie. Redcurrant jelly balances out the sharpness of the vinegar to give a scrumptious, rich tasting gravy that belies how simple it is to make.

1 Heat the oil in a large casserole pan. Cut the bacon into 1 cm (1/2 in) wide strips, and add to the pan.

2 Season the flour with salt and pepper and then toss the steak in the mixture. Shake off any excess flour and then add to the pan and cook for 7–8 minutes, turning from time to time until nicely browned.

3 Add the wine, pickled onions, redcurrant jelly and thyme. Bring to the boil, partially cover and simmer for 1 hour.

4 Preheat the oven to 200°C/400°F/Gas Mark 6. Open out the pastry and cut to about 2 cm (3/4 in) larger than the pan, rolling it out slightly more thinly if necessary. Place on top of the steak, tucking in the edges to enclose the filling. Brush with milk and then bake for 20 minutes, until golden and puffed.

GRAVY TIPS

BEN At home I always roast my meat and let it rest on a bed of vegetables for a great gravy base. This also stops the meat from burning. I use a good beef stock then thicken with gravy granules before passing it through a sieve for a fantastically smooth and tasty gravy.

PAUL The best restaurant gravy is a *jus*, basically a fantastic stew with the meat removed. But there are some short cuts. Brown some bones and meat trimmings, add a few root vegetables and a tomato. Pour in and reduce some red wine and then add the best shop-bought meat stock you can find. Cook slowly, pass through a strainer and you're left with a base for fantastic stews and gravies.

SILVANA You definitely need some meat residue for a fantastic gravy. If, like chicken, the meat's got a fatty residue I pour on a cold stock so the fat sets instantly, making it easy to skim off. I always add a splash of balsamic vinegar and a bit of redcurrant jelly for a balance of sharpness and sweetness.

SERVES 4

For the pan gritata:

4 tablespoons roughly chopped thyme leaves

4 tablespoons roughly chopped parsley

2 tablespoons roughly chopped marjoram

1 small dried-out or day-old ciabatta, made into rough crumbs

8 tablespoons sunflower oil

For the tomato sauce:

1 garlic clove, crushed

3 tablespoons olive oil

800 g jar of San Marzano plum tomatoes or 2 x 400 g cans of plum tomatoes in their own juice, drained

1–2 bird's eye chillies

500 g (1 lb 2 oz) pack best-quality durum wheat dried spaghetti

1 garlic clove, chopped

salt and freshly ground black pepper

Ben's

TOMATO AND HERB SPAGHETTI

Pasta is the most convenient food and people love it. This one I've cooked for staff meals in a busy kitchen. The key is to use good pasta and the best canned tomatoes. The best thing of all in this dish is the tasty crunch of the pan gritata – the herb and breadcrumb topping.

1 To make the pan gritata, first process the herbs in a food processor. Empty into a bowl, add the ciabatta crumbs and blend together using your hands.

2 Heat the sunflower oil in a frying pan and shallow-fry the herbs and breadcrumb mixture for 3–4 minutes, until crunchy. Drain on kitchen paper.

3 Make the tomato sauce by gently frying the garlic in 2 tablespoons of the olive oil for 30 seconds, until sticky. Add the tomatoes and chillies and cook for 30 minutes over a very low heat until broken down and the tartness has gone from the tomatoes.

4 Meanwhile, cook the pasta until al dente (according to the packet instructions) and drain. In a large frying pan, heat the remaining olive oil and add the chopped garlic. Toss through the cooked spaghetti. Then serve the spaghetti in a bowl with the tomato sauce surrounding it, and season with salt and freshly ground black pepper to taste. Sprinkle the pan gritata all over to serve.

3 BEST TOMATO SAUCE

BEN Simplicity is the key when it comes to tomato sauce. Use a really good quality San Marzano tomato, either tinned or jarred. Drain off the liquid. Finely slice some garlic, sauté in olive oil with the tomatoes and cook slowly. Then either eat it straight away or put it in a jar for later. Beautiful.

PAUL For me, the best tomato sauce is based on the Spanish romesco sauce. Really, really sun-sweetened, over-ripe tomatoes, maybe sprinkled with some saffron and some garlic and some thyme – roasted in the oven and then into a food blender with some of those fantastic dried Spanish peppers and perhaps a chilli. Whizz the whole thing up – irresistible.

SILVANA Start by frying a little bit of onion and garlic, then add tinned tomatoes. I like to add some meat on the bone (such as a lamb or pork chop), too, to give the sauce a fuller flavour. The odd sprig of herb sometimes goes in as well. But the key thing is to let it cook – a good hour for the flavours to develop into a nice rich sauce.

SERVES 4

450 g (1 lb) vine-ripened cherry tomatoes, left on the vine

1 kg (2 lb 4 oz) live clams

400 g (14 oz) garganelli or other dried pasta

100 ml (3½ fl oz) dry white wine

150 ml (5 fl oz) chicken stock

300 ml (10 fl oz) double cream

fresh wild garlic or basil leaves, torn

crusty bread, to serve

Paul's
GARGANELLI PASTA WITH CLAMS

At The Greenhouse, fresh pasta ravioli, rotolli and tortellini are always featured on the menu; however, at home, it is the simple pasta dishes that get the nod. Garganelli is a really rustic-looking version of penne pasta but the star of this dish is the fresh clams.

1 Preheat the oven to 150°C/325°F/Gas Mark 2. Place the tomatoes in a large baking tray. Roast for 1–1¼ hours, until the skins are wrinkled.

2 Meanwhile, prepare the shellfish. Scrub the clams, discarding any that are open or do not close when firmly tapped.

3 Cook the pasta in plenty of lightly salted water for 8 minutes or until al dente. Transfer to a colander and refresh under cold running water.

4 Add the clams to a large hot pan. Pour over the wine and chicken stock. Cover tightly and cook over a high heat, shaking the pan frequently, for 3–4 minutes, until the clams have steamed open. Any that have not opened at this stage should be discarded. Strain the clams through a colander, reserving the stock.

5 Pick two-thirds of the clams from their shells. Return the stock to the boil, add the cream and simmer for 5–6 minutes, until reduced slightly. Add the cold pasta and toss with the creamy sauce. Return all the clams to the pan, add the tomatoes and wild garlic or basil leaves. Serve with crusty bread.

Silvana's

CLASSIC SPAGHETTI CARBONARA

SERVES 2

250 g (9 oz) spaghetti
a knob of butter
140 g (5 oz) piece of pancetta, cubed
1 shallot, finely chopped
2 garlic cloves, finely chopped
2 eggs
150 ml (5 fl oz) single cream
small block Parmesan cheese, grated
salt and freshly ground black pepper

My all-time-favourite pasta dish – spaghetti carbonara – is notoriously tricky to make, but not if you follow this foolproof recipe. Just make sure you drain the pasta well and return it to the pan off the heat, there's enough heat retained in the hot pasta to thicken the eggs slightly but not too much to make them set to an unappetizing 'scrambled egg' consistency.

1 Cook the spaghetti in a large pan of boiling, salted water according to the instructions on the packet.

2 Melt the butter in a small frying pan. Add the pancetta and fry for 2 minutes, then add the shallot and garlic and cook for a further 3 minutes.

3 Lightly beat together the eggs and cream. Grate a large handful of Parmesan and beat into the cream mixture, with plenty of salt and pepper.

4 Drain the pasta well and quickly return to the pan. Add the bacon mixture and the cream mixture and toss well together so the heat from the pasta slightly thickens the sauce. Divide between two bowls and top with a good grinding of black pepper and a grating of Parmesan.

SERVES 4–6

1 small, stale ciabatta loaf

4 tablespoons olive oil

salt and freshly ground black pepper

For the tomato salad:

500 g (1 lb 2 oz) ripe vine tomatoes

a small bunch of fresh basil

2 garlic cloves

2 tablespoons white-wine vinegar

200 ml (7 fl oz) extra-virgin olive oil

salt and freshly ground black pepper

6 anchovy fillets, roughly chopped

about 100 g (4 oz) wide-leaf French rocket, washed

Ben's

CRUNCHY TOMATO PANZANELLA

This salad is a classic. Eat it alone, with grilled fish, scallops, squid or lamb – it's that versatile and the flavours sing!

1 Preheat oven to 200°C/400°F/Gas Mark 6. Cut the crusts from the bread and pull off long strips. Drizzle with olive oil and season with salt and pepper. Toast in the hot oven for 4–5 minutes until golden brown and crunchy on the outside but still soft in the middle.

2 Plunge the tomatoes into hot water, pour off the water, remove their skins and cut in half. Squeeze the seeds and juice from the tomato flesh over a sieve. Discard the seeds and retain the juice along with the flesh.

3 Rip the basil into pieces and put in pestle and mortar, with the cloves of garlic and a good pinch of salt. Pound to a pulp. Add the white-wine vinegar. Gradually add the olive oil and adjust the seasoning to taste.

4 Take the bread from the oven, put in a large bowl and add the tomato flesh and prepared dressing and toss around. Add the anchovies and rocket and serve.

Paul's

FIG, FETA AND SERRANO SALAD

This salad makes an appearance at The Greenhouse every summer. Search out black-skinned figs with ruby flesh and the finest Spanish Serrano ham (which for my money is superior to both Parma and Bayonne ham). The strong, salty feta is balanced perfectly by the sweetness of the figs and the peppery citrus dressing.

1 Whisk all the dressing ingredients together and adjust the seasoning to taste.

2 Trim the bases and separate the leaves from the Little Gem lettuces and the red chicory. Trim off just the very ends of the stalks of the watercress – much of that wonderful peppery flavour is in the stalks. Toss all the salad leaves together with 4 tablespoons of the dressing and arrange on individual serving plates.

3 Nestle the figs in the salad leaves and fold the Serrano ham into the salad. Add the feta cheese and serve with the remaining dressing to drizzle over.

SERVES 4

For the dressing:

150 ml (5 fl oz) extra-virgin olive oil

finely grated zest and juice of ½ a small lemon

1 teaspoon finely grated Parmesan cheese

1 teaspoon freshly ground black pepper

1 tablespoon snipped fresh chives

2 garlic cloves, finely chopped

a pinch of salt

1 teaspoon sherry vinegar

For the salad:

2 Little Gem lettuces

2 heads of red chicory

1 bunch of watercress, weighing about 50 g (2 oz)

1 bunch of dandelion leaves or rocket, weighing about 50 g (2 oz)

4 Black Mission figs (dark outside and red inside), quartered

6 slices Serrano ham, roughly torn

200 g (7 oz) block of Corsican or Greek feta cheese, broken into rough 1-inch cubes

3 BEST VINAIGRETTE TIPS

BEN It's about using really good olive oils, really good vinegars or just half-lemons, squeezed. Always add the acid first, so it coats the leaves, and then olive oil and salt and pepper; that way you get a really nice balance of flavours.

PAUL I prefer cider vinegar because I think it has quite a mellow flavour. I use it with a dollop of mustard and then just caster sugar and a little bit of salt and pepper whisked in, emulsifying the whole thing with a really light vegetable oil.

SILVANA When it comes to vinaigrettes, or any kind of dressing, I've only got one rule and that's twice the olive oil to vinegar. I'm not fussy about my vinegar – I use whatever I've got in my cupboard (not malt of course!).

SERVES 2

200 g (7 oz) orecchiette or other pasta shape

splash of olive oil

a large bunch of fresh flatleaf parsley

1 fresh rosemary sprig

1 garlic clove

1 red chilli, seeded and roughly chopped

6 sunblush tomatoes, roughly chopped

small block Parmesan cheese, finely grated

4 tablespoons extra-virgin olive oil

400 g can of butterbeans

salt and freshly ground black pepper

PASTA BUTTERBEAN SALAD

You have to go a long way to beat a home-made pesto and its flavour is well matched in this dish by the creaminess of the butterbeans. This pesto is made with parsley, so it has a mild flavour, but traditionalists can replace it with basil.

1 Cook the pasta according to packet instructions. Rinse in cold water, toss in a splash of olive oil and leave to cool.

2 Place the parsley, rosemary, garlic, chilli and tomatoes in a food processor. Whizz until finely chopped.

3 Add the Parmesan to the food processor with the olive oil and blitz again to form a rough paste. Add salt and pepper, to taste.

4 Drain the butterbeans and rinse well with cold water. Place in a large bowl with the cooked pasta and the pesto and toss well together. Serve at room temperature.

SERVES 4

For the curry paste:

5 long fresh chillies

5 red Thai shallots

4 garlic cloves

3 coriander roots

1 teaspoon salt

1 tablespoon good-quality curry powder

For the laksa:

500 ml (18 fl oz) coconut cream

2 tablespoons thick soy sauce

500 g (1 lb 2 oz) boneless, skinless chicken thigh meat

700 ml (1¼ pints) good chicken stock

1–2 teaspoons Thai fish sauce, to taste

To garnish:

500 g (1 lb 2 oz) dried ho fun rice noodles

1 tablespoon sunflower oil

4 garlic cloves, sliced

4 red Thai shallots, sliced

4 long dried chillies

¼ teaspoon salt

1 teaspoon caster sugar

1–2 limes, halved

1 small head of chicory, roughly chopped

100 g (4 oz) beansprouts

4 tablespoons chopped fresh coriander

Ben's

CHICKEN AND NOODLE LAKSA

Time and again, my tastebuds get the need for an Asian fix and noodles are one hell of a way to satisfy my need. This is something I love to eat, especially when I travel back home to Perth. The stopover in Malaysia is just an excuse to have what I consider the best noodle dish in the world – laksa. I've added a little Thai touch here, with my crunchy seasoning and, once you've had this, it'll be all you will ever want to eat.

1 Blitz all the curry paste ingredients together in a food processor to a coarse paste.

2 Pour the coconut cream into a large saucepan. Boil it over a medium heat until it separates. Add the curry paste and fry for 2–3 minutes, until fragrant.

3 Stir in the soy sauce and chicken and cook for 3–4 minutes, stirring occasionally. Add the chicken stock, bring to the boil and simmer gently for 20 minutes. Season to taste with fish sauce. Keep warm.

4 Meanwhile, arrange the noodles in a large bowl and pour over boiling water to cover. Leave to stand for 4 minutes, then drain.

5 Heat the sunflower oil in a frying pan and fry the sliced garlic, and separately fry the shallots and chillies for about 30 seconds until crispy and golden brown. Strain and cool. Pound together in a pestle and mortar with the salt and sugar.

6 Divide the drained noodles between four serving bowls. Top with chicken curry sauce. Serve with a garnish of limes, scatter with the garlic, shallot and chilli mix, chicory, beansprouts and coriander.

92

For the sweet and sour sauce:

600 ml (1 pint) water

150 ml (5 fl oz) malt vinegar

3 tomatoes, halved

4 cm (1½ in) piece of fresh root ginger, finely chopped

50 ml (2 fl oz) syrup from a jar of stem ginger

1 teaspoon soy sauce

1 tablespoon demerara sugar

1 teaspoon cornflour, mixed with 1 tablespoon tomato ketchup

Paul's

SWEET AND SOUR NOODLE CHOW-CHOW

I used to visit a small Nepalese restaurant in North London and, on one occasion, I asked the waiter to choose for me. I got chow-chow – a rich, smoky noodle dish which I've come somewhere close to recreating here. It's finished with a simple sweet and sour sauce served with some pan-fried bream.

1 Put all the sweet and sour sauce ingredients, except the cornflour and ketchup mixture, into a saucepan. Bring to the boil, then simmer for 25–30 minutes. Stir in the cornflour mixture and cook, stirring, until thickened and glossy.

2 Drop the noodles into a large pan of lightly salted boiling water, bring back to the boil and cook for 4 minutes. Drain and cool under cold water.

3 Heat the olive oil in a large frying pan and fry the bream, skin-side down, for 3–4 minutes. Turn and cook for about a further 2 minutes.

4 Meanwhile, heat half the mixed oils in a large frying pan or wok, add the cold, drained noodles and stir-fry until lightly coloured. Transfer to a plate and keep warm. Then add the remaining oil to the wok and stir-fry the vegetables for 2 minutes, starting with the mushrooms and sweetcorn, then adding the pepper, garlic and ginger, then the spring onions, mangetout and finally the carrots. Add the noodles, sweet and sour sauce, coriander, fish sauce and soy sauce to taste and mix well. Serve with the pan-fried bream.

For the noodles:

500 g pack of 4-minute dried medium egg noodles

1 tablespoon sesame oil and 1 tablespoon vegetable oil, mixed

4 shiitake mushrooms, sliced

4 baby sweetcorn, quartered lengthways

1/2 red and 1/2 yellow pepper, cut into thin strips

1 garlic clove, finely chopped

2.5 cm (1 in) piece of fresh root ginger, peeled and finely chopped

2 spring onions, cut into 4 cm (1 1/2 in) pieces

6 mangetout

1 carrot, cut into thin matchsticks

3 tablespoons chopped fresh coriander

1 teaspoon Thai fish sauce (nam pla)

1 teaspoon soy sauce

For the bream:

1 tablespoon olive oil

4 bream fillets, skin on, weighing about 150–175 g (5–6 oz) each

Silvana's

ORIENTAL NOODLE SALAD

SERVES 2

100 g (4 oz) glass vermicelli noodles

2 tablespoons red-wine vinegar

1/2 teaspoon salt

1/2 teaspoon caster sugar

1 small red onion

1 mini cucumber

1 red bird's eye chilli, finely chopped, seeds and all

75 g (2^3/$_4$ oz) smoked salmon, torn into shreds

small handful of fresh coriander leaves

1 tablespoon sesame seeds

Now this may sound like a slightly odd combination but the lightly pickled vegetables are complemented brilliantly by the smoked salmon. No added oil makes this a great healthy choice – ideal for the-morning-after or to kickstart a detox.

1 Place the noodles in a large heatproof bowl, cover with boiling water and set aside for 5 minutes or so.

2 In a separate, large bowl, mix together the vinegar, salt and sugar. Thinly slice the red onion and add to the bowl.

3 Lightly peel the cucumber, allowing a few slivers of green skin to remain. Halve the cucumber lengthways, then using a teaspoon, scoop out and discard the seeds. Thinly slice the cucumber, slightly on a diagonal to give slanted half-moon shapes, then place in the bowl. Stir in the chillies, smoked salmon and coriander leaves.

4 Drain the noodles and cool under running water. Add to the bowl and toss well together.

5 Lightly toast the sesame seeds in a small, non-stick pan. Divide the noodle mixture between two bowls and sprinkle the toasted sesame seeds over the top.

96

SERVES 4

4 bulbs of round, firm, female Florence fennel

3 tablespoons olive oil

100 ml (3½ fl oz) still mineral water

2 garlic cloves, finely chopped

salt and freshly ground black pepper

Ben's

STEAMED FLORENCE FENNEL

I first cooked this at the River Café and my girlfriend loves it. It's a great way to enjoy fennel. Use it as a side dish for lamb or fish, or enjoy it on grilled bruschetta or as a part of a vegetable antipasto. It's so easy to do. Make sure you use female fennel bulbs which are more rounded and have a fuller flavour.

1 Trim the feathery tops from each fennel bulb, chop them and reserve for garnishing, then cut each bulb into eighths.

2 Heat 2 tablespoons of the olive oil in a large, shallow saucepan. Add the fennel and sauté until it begins to colour golden brown.

3 Add a splash of mineral water to create steam and continue to cook until the water evaporates. Repeat this process until the fennel is very soft but still holds its shape. It should be a rich brown colour.

4 Stir in the garlic and cook for 1 minute, until softened. Drizzle with the remaining olive oil and scatter with the reserved fennel tops. Season to taste.

Paul's PERFECT PEPPERONATA

Here is a really versatile vegetable side dish, packed full of Mediterranean flavour. Serve it warm with chicken, fish or pasta, or cold as a relish. Choose the ripest tomatoes available and make it a little in advance as it just gets better and better. How did this get beaten by a bowl of brown fennel?!

1 Heat half the olive oil in a large, shallow saucepan and sauté the onion over a low heat for 1–2 minutes, until softened slightly but not coloured.

2 Stir in the saffron, dried chilli and garlic and sauté for a further 1 minute.

3 Add the peppers, stir well and cook for 3–4 minutes, until just beginning to soften.

4 Add the remaining olive oil to the pan and stir in the tomatoes, sugar and seasoning. Cook gently over a low heat for up to 1 hour, stirring occasionally.

SERVES 2

4 tablespoons good olive oil

a large brown-skinned Spanish onion, cut in half and thinly sliced

a pinch of saffron threads

a pinch of flaked dried red chillies

1 garlic clove, sliced

1 red pepper, cut in half, seeded and sliced

1 yellow pepper, cut in half, seeded and sliced

6 ripe vine tomatoes, roughly chopped

a pinch of sugar

salt and freshly ground black pepper

3 BEST SALT & PEPPER TIPS

BEN I love flavouring salts myself. Celery salt is one of my favourites. Just pound and dry in a slow oven. It's versatile and great with fish and meat. When it comes to pepper I do like to use soft green peppercorns in cream sauces and especially with steak.

PAUL When it comes to pepper I always grind white peppercorns because white pepper is as effective as black and doesn't show, especially in sauces and soups. For most seasoning I prefer table salt – it breaks down straight away – and it's economical. If you're serving raw fish like salmon, a mixture of rock salt and sugar will draw out moisture and has great preserving qualities.

SILVANA I love sea salt for its texture as well as seasoning qualities. A sprinkle of crystals makes simple things like chips or fried egg really special. But if I'm just using salt to cook pasta, ordinary table salt will do. I use black pepper with everything, always whole, grinding it as and when I need it.

3 BEST ROAST POTATO TIPS

BEN It's got to be Maris Piper for the fluffiest roast potatoes. For the best effect, I rough them up in a colander after parboiling and then roast them with sunflower oil, sage and rosemary for added flavour.

PAUL For me, new potatoes make the best roasties in summer. I parboil and then leave them to dry before peeling the skin off and roasting them in duck fat, thyme and garlic for fantastic flavour.

SILVANA Desirée red-skinned potatoes are my favourite because they hold their shape well and I like to roast them in the Italian way. Cut them into quarters always before tossing them in olive oil, oregano and salt. I use a non-stick roasting tin and don't turn them too much during cooking for fabulously firm roasties.

Silvana's
ROASTED ASPARAGUS

When it comes to asparagus, I like to keep it simple. Whenever possible go for nice thick English asparagus, in season for a few weeks only during the late spring or early summer.

1 Preheat the oven to 220°C/425°F/Gas Mark 7. Snap off the woody ends of the asparagus spears and peel from the base to about half way up the stem.

2 Place on a baking sheet in a single layer, dot with butter, drizzle with balsamic vinegar and sprinkle with the sugar and sea salt.

3 Roast for 8–10 minutes, until just cooked through. Serve immediately.

SERVES 4

a bunch of thick English asparagus
(about 12 spears)

25 g (1 oz) butter

1 teaspoon balsamic vinegar

1/2 teaspoon caster sugar

coarse sea salt

Ben's

CHINESE PORK AND EGG CONGEE

Saturday nights after a hard evening in the restaurant kitchen (or Sunday nights after an even harder night in the pub) always involved this speciality Chinese dish. Congee, a nourishing rice porridge, can be served in so many ways but this is my favourite; the judges loved it and it's so easy to make.

1 Wash the rice in several changes of water and soak overnight in 850 ml (1½ pints) of water, with the oil and salt. Drain well the next day.

2 To make the congee, bring the chicken stock to the boil in a saucepan and add the soaked rice. Bring to the boil and simmer very gently for 2 hours, until it breaks down. Check the seasoning and keep warm.

3 Meanwhile, cook the eggs. Put them into cold, salted water, bring to the boil and cook for 8 minutes. Refresh in cold water. Roll until the shells crack, but are not coming off.

SERVES 4

For the congee:

140 g (5 oz) fragrant long-grain Thai rice

1 tablespoon sunflower oil

1 teaspoon salt

2 litres (3$^{1}/_{2}$ pints) fresh chicken stock

3 duck or chicken eggs

150 ml (5 fl oz) dark soy sauce, plus extra to serve

2 star anise

2 tablespoons green gunpowder tea

For the Chinese Pork:

1 tablespoon Szechuan pepper

1 teaspoon salt

350 g (12 oz) pork fillet

1 teaspoon vegetable oil

To serve:

2 spring onions, very thinly sliced

a handful of prawn crackers, crumbled

freshly ground white pepper

4 Put the eggs back in the pan. Add the soy sauce and enough water to cover, with the star anise and green tea. Bring to the boil and simmer for a further 1$^{1}/_{2}$ hours. Leave to cool in the liquid until needed.

5 Preheat the oven to 200°C/400°F/Gas Mark 6. In a pestle and mortar, crush the Szechuan pepper and salt and sprinkle over a plate. Roll the pork fillet in the mixture to coat. Heat the oil over a high heat in a small ovenproof frying pan and seal the pork quickly, without colouring. Transfer to the oven and roast for about 12–15 minutes, until medium to well done. Allow to rest for a few minutes and then slice thinly.

6 To finish, peel the eggs and cut them in half. Carefully stir them through the congee, with the sliced pork. Heat the mixture through gently for a few minutes. Spoon into serving bowls and top with the spring onions and crumbled prawn crackers. Drizzle over some more soy sauce and a grinding of white pepper. Serve at once.

Paul's PAELLA

Spain is culinarily an important country; fantastic ingredients, some of the world's leading chefs and this classic peasant dish. Many versions exist, so here's mine. Look for calaspara rice and good-quality saffron. And finally (unless you have Silvana around for dinner) don't leave out the snails.

1 Heat the olive oil in a paella pan or large, shallow frying pan and sauté the garlic for 1 minute.

2 Add the rabbit and chicken breast and lightly brown over a high heat for about 5 minutes, turning once or twice. Add the prawns and mussels.

3 Sprinkle over the chopped tomatoes and allow to soften for a minute, shaking the pan now and again (don't be tempted to stir the paella). Sprinkle over the rice and the saffron.

4 Pour over the chicken stock, shaking the pan to disperse. Drop in the cannellini beans, snails, frozen broad beans and peas and paprika to taste. Simmer for 15–20 minutes, shaking the pan every so often, but not stirring.

5 Five minutes before the end of cooking time, add the cherry tomatoes. Season to taste and serve at once.

SERVES 3–4

1 tablespoon extra-virgin olive oil

2 garlic cloves, thinly sliced

1 saddle of rabbit, cut into even-sized pieces

1 chicken breast, cut into large chunks

4 raw king prawns, shell on

10–15 live mussels, washed and debearded (see page 48)

4 ripe vine tomatoes, finely chopped

200 g (7 oz) Spanish paella rice

a large pinch of saffron

1 litre (1³/₄ pints) hot chicken stock, fresh or from a cube

200 g (7 oz) canned cannellini beans, drained and rinsed

10 canned snails

50 g (2 oz) frozen broad beans

50 g (2 oz) frozen peas

paprika to taste

10 cherry tomatoes

salt and freshly ground black pepper

Silvana's
CRUSTY SQUASH PILAF

SERVES 4

1 teaspoon golden caster sugar

a large pinch of saffron strands

50 g (2 oz) butter

450 g (1 lb) basmati rice

2 tablespoons vegetable oil

1 large onion, thinly sliced

1 red-skin potato, weighing about 250 g (9 oz), cubed

1 small butternut squash, peeled, seeded and cubed

1 bird's eye chilli

1 cinnamon stick

salt

For the cucumber drizzle:

8 cm (3 in) piece of cucumber, peeled and cut into chunks

1 garlic clove, roughly chopped

a small handful of coriander, mint or, ideally, a mixture of both

4 tablespoons natural yoghurt

a squeeze of fresh lemon or lime juice

This is inspired by the classic Indian restaurant dish 'Persian Rice'. As such it's not spicy but instead very fragrant with a tiny touch of sweetness. As it cooks slowly, the rice crisps up on the base, giving a lovely mixture of textures. Delicious and foolproof!

1 Place the sugar, saffron, butter and 2 tablespoons of water in a ramekin or teacup and microwave for 1 minute until the butter melts. Set aside to infuse. Alternatively, cook on the hob in a small pan.

2 Rinse the rice in a sieve using warm water. Add the rice to a pan of boiling, salted water and cook for exactly 5 minutes. It should be nearly done but still slightly hard in the centre.

3 Meanwhile, heat the vegetable oil in a large flame-proof casserole. Add the onion to the pan with the potato and squash. Cook for 5 minutes or so over a high heat, until beginning to brown. Chop the chilli, seeds and all, and add to the pan. Turn off the heat.

4 Spoon half of the vegetable mixture out of the casserole into a bowl. Spoon half of the saffron mixture into the pan, over the vegetables. Top with half of the rice, then the reserved vegetables and then the remainder of the rice. Drizzle over the remaining saffron mixture; then break the cinnamon stick on top.

5 Cover the pan tightly and cook over the lowest heat for 30 minutes, until the rice is completely tender and has formed a golden crust on the bottom.

6 While the rice cooks, place the cucumber, garlic and herbs in a small food processor with some salt and whizz until smooth. Add the yoghurt and a squeeze of lemon juice and whizz again to make a thin, frothy sauce. Serve alongside the rice.

SERVES 6

For the pastry cases:

175 g (6 oz) plain flour

85 g (3 oz) frozen unsalted butter, diced

50 g (2 oz) icing sugar

1 egg yolk

For the filling:

2 eggs

4 egg yolks

100 ml (3¹/₂ fl oz) pink grapefruit juice (about 2 grapefruit)

finely grated zest and juice of 1 small lemon

140 g (5 oz) cold unsalted butter, cubed

100 g (4 oz) caster sugar

Ben's

PINK GRAPEFRUIT TART

Summer's a wonderful time for fruit and there are so many to choose from to fill a summer-time tart. Lemons are so often used and are great but I'm always up for something different. So here I've used a much neglected summer citrus fruit, the bitter-sweet pink grapefruit. It's a wonderful way to end a meal and cleanse the palate. Definitely worth giving it a go… and grating the frozen pastry straight into the tart tins is a really quick alternative to rolling it!

1 Blitz the flour, butter and icing sugar in a food processor to fine breadcrumbs. Stir in the egg yolk until well combined and the pastry starts to come together to a soft dough. Divide the pastry into six equal-size pieces. Freeze until firm.

2 Preheat the oven to 180°C/350°F/Gas Mark 4. Grate the pastry into 10 cm (4 in) straight-sided, loose-bottomed tart tins, which are 2.5 cm (1 in) deep. Press the pastry evenly into the base and up the sides of the tins. Bake for about 15 minutes, until golden brown.

3 Next, prepare the filling. Whisk the eggs and egg yolks together. Place in a saucepan with the grapefruit juice, lemon zest and juice, butter and sugar and cook over a low heat, stir-ring continuously until the mixture has thickened and coats the back of the spoon. It should be a thick custard. Pour into the cooked pastry cases and allow to set.

4 Put the tarts on a baking tray and bake for about 8 minutes, until golden brown. Remove from the tins and serve at room temperature, with crème fraîche and dusted with icing sugar.

To serve:
200 g carton of crème fraîche
icing sugar, to dust

Paul's
PLUM BAKLAVA TART

SERVES 4

12 ripe black plums, stoned
and quartered

85 g (3 oz) caster sugar

50 g (2 oz) walnuts

2 tablespoons demerara sugar

1/4 teaspoon ground cinnamon

1/4 teaspoon ground ginger

6 large sheets of filo pastry

85 g (3 oz) butter, melted

To serve:

vanilla ice-cream

Baklava has always been a favourite of mine; I've used the filo, walnuts, sugar and spice combination in many ways, but perhaps to best effect with this baklava filo tart shell. If plums aren't available, use peaches, figs or apricots, or just fill the tarts with ice-cream.

1 Preheat the oven to 190°C/375°F/Gas Mark 5.

2 Make the tart filling by cooking the plums with the sugar for 10–12 minutes, until the plums are soft but still holding their shape.

3 Meanwhile, put the walnuts, demerara sugar, cinnamon and ginger into a food processor and process until fine.

4 Cut the filo pastry into 12 equal-sized squares (3 per tart). (Each square must be large enough to fit comfortably within the individual baking ring in which it will be cooked, with some overhang.) Lay one square of filo on the work surface, brush with melted butter and sprinkle it with the walnut mixture. Then place another square on top, offset to create a star shape. Butter it, sprinkle with the walnut mixture again, and lay a third square on top, again offset. Repeat this process to make another three filo sandwiches.

5 Place four baking rings on a baking tray. Place each pastry sandwich over a baking ring and push the centre of the pastry square gently down into the ring, allowing the points of the pastry to stick up. Place a ball of tin foil in the middle of each tart and bake for 5–8 minutes until just beginning to colour.

6 Remove the pastry cases to individual serving plates and spoon in the plum mixture. Serve immediately, with a ball of ice-cream on top.

SERVES 6

500 g carton of mascarpone cheese

4 tablespoons icing sugar, plus extra
to serve

4 pieces of stem ginger

250 g punnet of fresh raspberries

6 round shortbread biscuits

RASPBERRY CHEESECAKE TART

Yes really, you can make this perfect dinner-party pudding in under 10 minutes. Try this with other soft berries, such as diced strawberries or blackberries.

1 Spoon the mascarpone into a large bowl. Sift over the icing sugar.

2 Finely chop the ginger and stir into the mascarpone, along with a handful of the raspberries. At this stage, the mixture can be chilled until ready to serve.

3 To assemble, place the shortbreads on a board. Using a flexible 30 cm (12 in) ruler or similarly sized strip of plastic, form a circle around one piece of shortbread, securing the ends with tape.

4 Spoon one-sixth of the mixture into the ring, roughly levelling off the surface. Undo the tape and remove the plastic. Repeat with the remaining shortcakes.

5 Scatter the rest of the raspberries over the top of each, with a pinch or two of icing sugar.

Ben's

SUMMER BERRY COMPOTE

200 g (7 oz) caster sugar

1 vanilla pod, split

1–2 teaspoons freshly ground black pepper, to taste

175 ml (6 fl oz) Valpolicella red wine

600 g (1lb 5 oz) mixed summer fruits, e.g. strawberries, raspberries, blueberries, blackberries, etc

1 tablespoon chopped fresh basil

200 g carton of thick Greek yoghurt

The base of this delicious dessert is one I normally use to make a fantastic summer pudding, but instead of waiting 24 hours for the summer pudding to soak, I love to enjoy this fresh alternative immediately with a good dollop of Greek yoghurt. Give it a go!

1 Sprinkle 140 g (5 oz) of the sugar into a heavy-based saucepan. Pour over 50 ml (2 fl oz) water and stir to make a paste. Cook to a light golden caramel.

2 Add the split vanilla pod, some ground black pepper and the red wine and bring to the boil. Simmer until reduced by half. Remove from the heat and gently stir in the fruit. Leave to stand until cold before spooning into glasses.

3 Put the remaining caster sugar and the basil into a mortar and grind with the pestle until combined and the mixture is fine and dry. Add more sugar if the mixture is still wet.

4 Drop spoonfuls of the Greek yoghurt over the fruit and sprinkle with the basil sugar just before serving.

3 BEST

CHOPPING TIPS

BEN Think 'evenly' when you are chopping. Cut your vegetables into the same-sized pieces, then they'll cook in the same time. Use a big knife for the big jobs and, for herbs, I use a *mezza luna* (half-moon-shaped rocking chopper). Never sharpen your knives with a steel – it will only smooth the edge, not sharpen the blade. I like to use a stone.

PAUL A sharp knife is really important because it makes a clean cut and all the juices from the fruit or vegetables do not seep out on to the board to be wasted. It's not just the size of the knife that matters, it's also the size of the board. Make sure it's big enough for the job in hand.

SILVANA Use a knife that you can handle. Don't try to copy the professionals, just take your time. When you're chopping root vegetables, keep the root on – it makes them far easier to chop. I always test my knife first to make sure it's sharp. I just run it along a tomato and, if it slices the surface, you know it's going to do the job.

Paul's

PEACH AND RASPBERRY CLAFOUTIS

One of my dessert-island sweets – total bliss and oh so easy! I've used the vanilla, raspberry and peach melba combination here, but, classically, clafoutis features soured cherries. Blueberries work well, as do cooked, spiced apple and sultanas. Whatever the fruit, give it a go. Even my kids love it!

1 Preheat the oven to 180°C/350°F/Gas Mark 4. Whisk the eggs and caster sugar with an electric whisk until thick and the mixture holds its own shape (this will take about 10 minutes and the mixture is now called a sabayon).

2 Lightly whip the cream and fold into the sabayon. Fold in the flour and ground almonds and carefully stir in the seeds of one vanilla pod.

3 If the peaches are very ripe, the skins should come off easily. If not, drop the peaches into boiling water for 20 seconds. Remove and plunge into cold water. Cut a small nick in the top of each peach and slip off the skins.

4 Cut the peaches into chunks and divide between four individual oven-proof dishes. Add the raspberries, pour over the clafoutis batter and bake for approximately 10–12 minutes, until golden. Serve with vanilla ice-cream and dusted with icing sugar.

SERVES 4

4 eggs

140 g (5 oz) caster sugar

300 ml (10 fl oz) double cream

1 tablespoon plain white flour

1/2 tablespoon ground almonds

1 vanilla pod

2 peaches

16 raspberries

To serve:

vanilla ice-cream

icing sugar

Silvana's

STRAWBERRY MARGARITA GRANITA

SERVES 4

50 g (2 oz) caster sugar

400 g (14 oz) strawberries

4 limes

100 ml (3½ fl oz) tequila

50 ml (2 fl oz) orange liqueur, Triple Sec, Cointreau or Grand Marnier

A frozen cocktail for pudding? I can't think of anything more tempting or exciting but this contains as much alcohol as you'd expect to find in a cocktail, so be careful, it's very potent.

1 Place the sugar in a pan with 150 ml (5 fl oz) water and heat gently, stirring until the sugar dissolves. Remove from the heat and set aside to cool.

2 Hull and halve the strawberries and place in a liquidizer or food processor. Squeeze in the juice from three of the limes and whizz until smooth. Pass the strawberry mixture through a fine strainer into the cooled syrup then stir in the tequila and orange liqueur.

3 Pour the mixture into a shallow container and freeze for 3 hours. This grainy frozen mixture is called granita. Thinly slice the remaining lime, place on a sheet of plastic wrap and freeze.

4 Scrape the surface of the granita with a spoon to loosen the crystals. Spoon into four tumblers, slipping in the lime slices as you go. Serve immediately. Alternatively, break up the mixture with a fork and then return to the freezer until ready to serve.

SERVES 8

1.2 litres (2 pints) double cream

2 vanilla pods, split

finely grated zest of 1 unwaxed lemon

3 gelatine leaves

150 ml (5 fl oz) full-fat milk

250 g (9 oz) good-quality white chocolate

85 g (3 oz) icing sugar

fresh strawberries, aged balsamic vinegar and icing sugar, to serve

Ben's

WHITE CHOCOLATE PANNACOTTA

White chocolate is the sexiest chocolate you can get. Its subtle vanilla characteristic blends so well with the delicate, melt-in-your-mouth texture of this Italian set-cream custard. Matching it with the most amazing combination of ripe strawberries and aged balsamic makes for a blow-out dessert.

1 Pour 900 ml (1²/₃ pints) of the double cream into a small pan and stir in the vanilla pods and lemon zest. Then simmer until reduced by a quarter. Keep warm.

2 Soak the gelatine in the cold milk to soften. Then warm the milk until the gelatine is dissolved. Stir into the reduced cream mixture, along with the white chocolate. Pass through a sieve into a bowl and chill over ice until thickened but not solid.

3 Lightly whip the remaining double cream and fold in the icing sugar. Fold this mixture into the thickened white-chocolate cream. Divide between eight cappuccino cups (about 150 ml (5 fl oz) capacity) and leave to set. To serve, turn each pannacotta out onto a plate and top with quartered fresh strawberries, which have been slightly crushed with a little icing sugar, and drizzle with balsamic vinegar.

Paul's
CLASSIC CHOCOLATE FONDANT

SERVES 8

A small knob of butter, softened

cocoa powder, for dusting

140 g (5 oz) best-quality 65–70% bitter chocolate

140 g (5 oz) unsalted butter

3 large free-range eggs

3 large free-range egg yolks

85 g (3 oz) caster sugar

100 g (4 oz) plain white flour

For the choc-chip cream:

300 ml (10 fl oz) double cream, stiffly whipped

runny honey, to taste

100 g (4 oz) milk chocolate, grated

A fantastic chocolate dessert found on many restaurant menus (including mine!). Easy to make and a joy to eat. The secret here is to find a good quality chocolate of at least 65% cocoa solids. At The Greenhouse restaurant, we serve it with home-made peanut-butter ice-cream, but vanilla works just as well or give my milk-choc-chip cream a go! Just imagine pushing the spoon through the soft chocolate crust and finding an oozing chocolate filling.

1 Preheat the oven to 180°C/350°F/Gas Mark 4. Butter eight 150 ml (5 fl oz) ramekins and dust with cocoa powder to coat.

2 Melt the chocolate and butter in a bowl over a pan of simmering water until thick and glossy.

3 Whisk the whole eggs, egg yolks and sugar in a large bowl with an electric whisk for 6–8 minutes, until thick and creamy and the mixture holds its shape. Pour the melted chocolate over the egg mixture and sift over the flour. Carefully fold in, using a large metal spoon. Divide the mixture between the ramekins, leaving a 1 cm (1/2 in) space at the top of each ramekin to allow the fondants to rise. Bake for 9–10 minutes.

4 While the fondants are cooking, make the choc-chip cream by mixing together the whipped cream, honey to taste and grated milk chocolate.

5 Remove the fondants from oven and turn out on to individual serving plates. (They should turn out of the ramekins very easily; however, if you get one that sticks a little, simply run a sharp knife around the edge.) Serve at once with the choc-chip cream.

CHEF'S TIP
This pudding can be made up to 1 hour in advance.

150 ml (5 fl oz) double cream

4 cardamom pods, cracked

150 g (5½ oz) of good-quality milk chocolate

Vanilla ice-cream and Italian biscuits, to serve

Silvana's

SPEEDY CARDAMOM CHOCOLATE SAUCE

Forget cocoa, real chocolate sauce needs real milk chocolate. I use this sauce in lots of different ways but I love it most served hot with ice-cream and some crunchy biscuits. Any leftovers, once cooled, make a great chocolate spread. Oh, and try switching the cream for triple the quantity of milk for the world's best drinking chocolate.

1 Place the cream in a heatproof jug. Crack the cardamom pods in a pestle and mortar, removing the husks. Lightly crush the seeds and add the seeds to the cream and heat in a microwave on high for 1 minute; alternatively, heat in a small pan until it begins to boil and then remove from the heat.

2 Break the chocolate into small pieces. Stir into the hot cream, mixing until smooth.

3 Place a scoopful of ice-cream in four small glass bowls, pour over the hot sauce and serve with the biscuits on the side.

CHEF'S TIP
Whatever happens, once you begin to add the chocolate to the cream don't put it back in the microwave or it will become very thick. Providing that the cream hits boiling point, there will be enough heat to melt the chocolate.

ACKNOWLEDGEMENTS

All our thanks to everyone at Endemol UK and all involved in the production and filming for giving us the opportunity to make what we consider to be a fantastic show. Here goes: Lovely Sue, Janice, Baz, Stuart, Claudia, Karen, Sharon, Scarlett & Christine, Lesley, Clare McG, Sarah, Clare M, Natasha, Doug, Chris, Silver Fox, Fox Cub, Kevin, Andy, Ben, Jay, Anna and Monica. Thanks to all at BBC Books, Nicky, Rachel and Julia for all your cheerful encouragement in pulling the book together, to the polite, patient and talented Gareth Morgans for taking such gorgeous photographs, and to our food stylist David Morgan for staying calm, managing to control all three of us and helping to achieve such appetizing results.

Silvana
Firstly, plenty of love to my boys Ben and Paul. I've been incredibly lucky to have been given a chance to work alongside you two in what turned out to be such a brilliant experience. I've enjoyed almost every minute of it and learned absolutely loads along the way – I will be calling into your restaurants for my tea on a monthly basis, just to make sure you've still got my *Mushy Pea Fishcakes* (Paul) and *Raspberry Cheesecake Tart* (Ben) on the menu. Love and thanks of course go to my best girls at Fork, Jenny, Angela and Kim, for putting up with weeks of not being able to get into your own kitchen and all the chaos that comes with a film crew, but mostly for being constantly supportive – I'm very lucky to have you. Many thanks to Rob for cheerfully picking me up, tired and grumpy after filming, and making my tea every night when I couldn't cook any more, and also for laughing so heartily at every weak gag ever made on the show. And finally, thanks to my smashing agents Sarah and Jerry.

Ben
Thank you first of all to my co-conspirators Silvana and Paul. Thank you also to my girlfriend De-arne for all her patience and loving encouragement, and my staff at Monte's for their hard work and commitment to excellence, without which I wouldn't have been able to do the show or the book. Thank you to Martine @ dml for all her hard work to get me these wonderful opportunities. A big up to all my mates north and south of the equator and a 'THIS ONE IS FOR YOU' to my mum and dad, granny and bro Daniel, and a big thank you to any one else I may have forgotten.

Paul
Major thanks to: Ben and Silvana for allowing me to win (at least occasionally); Joe Levin for smiling kindly throughout the whole ordeal; everyone at The Greenhouse restaurant, especially James, Todd, Glen and Damo for covering up any absence (perhaps a little too efficiently!); and, most importantly, MJ, Ellie and Richie for belief beyond belief.

INDEX